P9-CJU-711

there are no rules, only imagination

ANNE McKEVITT'S StyleSolutions

365 OF THE freshest looks, smartest tips & best advice FOR YOUR HOME

Anne McKevitt

Clarkson Potter/Publishers
New York

The author, the company, and the publishers take no responsibility for injury or loss arising from the procedures or use of materials described in this book. Materials, tools, skills, and work areas vary greatly and are the responsibility of the reader. Follow manufacturers' instructions and take appropriate safety precautions. Always ensure that children's products are child-safe and nontoxic. When using candles, never place them near flammable materials or leave them unattended, always be aware of the fire hazard, and ensure that they are used safely.

Published by Clarkson Potter/Publishers, New York, New York.
Member of the Crown Publishing Group, a division of Random House, Inc.
www.randomhouse.com

Printed in the United States of America

Library of Congress Cataloging-in-Publication Data is available upon request.

ISBN 1-4000-4610-6

10 9 8 7 6 5 4 3 2 1

First Edition

Creating a book is never a singlehanded event by the author, and I feel it's important to recognize the talents of those who made *Style Solutions* possible:

From the Anne McKevitt Ideas team extra-special thanks to Matt Giannasi, Laura Hunter, Annabelle Grundy, Will Hutchinson, Elise Jamieson, Becky Reynolds, and Jess Albert. Thanks also to Janet Hunter for loaning many props.

To everyone at Clarkson Potter– in particular, Lauren Shakely, Katie Workman, Marysarah Quinn, and Caitlin Daniels Israel.

To Colin Poole for his beautiful photography.

Lastly, to Don, for absolutely everything, and to Sooty and Bagpuss for being purrfect cat models.

contents

GLASS CLOTH

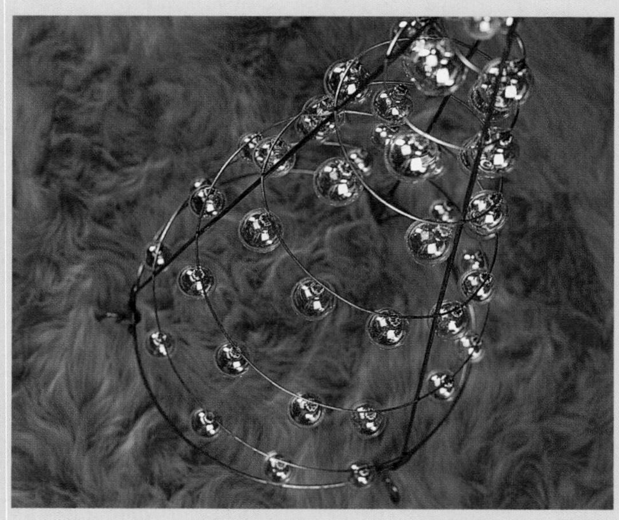

STARBUCKS COFFEE
Classic
FREE PARTY BUCKS INSIDE!

introduction

This book is aimed at real people who lead real lives—for those who don't have the time or the inclination after rushing in from the office or picking the kids up from school to make hors d'oeuvres. This book gives you my frank, no-nonsense approach to fabulous style solutions for your home. Whether it's adding extra touches with spectacular small details, dreaming up innovative larger decorating schemes, or creating magical seasonal events or gorgeous gifts, time plays a factor. I realize that, just like me, you probably only have five to ten minutes to set the table before family and friends arrive for a celebratory meal, or only a free weekend to jazz up your entire bedroom with a new color scheme. I understand your time constraints and money restraints. Just like you, I'm also pushed for time and I don't want to break the bank.

Thinking about creating the home you want can be very daunting, or so you may have been led to think by other out-of-step decorating purists. The old way of thinking is that the longer you toil over something the better the finished result. I couldn't disagree more with this—it's completely ridiculous. In truth everyone, given encouraging, sensible suggestions, rather than ironclad dictatorial instructions, can discover the confidence to turn the mundane into the magnificent. From the smallest object to the biggest project, you can take on all kinds of decorating projects in a realistic amount of time.

I am a great believer in flexibility. Real life is not a rigid construction and neither is decorating. You should feel that you can improvise on anything in this book, as you see different ways to make it easier to achieve or appropriate for a different location. The more time saved doing any project, the more time you have to put your feet up and enjoy the finished result; and the more you think about design in general, broad strokes of inspiration, rather than inflexible room-by-room projects, the more your creative juices will flow.

Professional decorators and designers rely on relatively large budgets and an army of support. As a professional myself, I too have had this experience, but when I got started as a self-taught designer I had to do everything myself. In this book I draw on my early experiences to help you so that you don't make some of the mistakes I have made myself. This book is like having me beside you while you work away at your latest creation—not snapping instructions but gently coaxing you along with easy-to-follow how-tos and a multitude of invaluable tips. Enjoy this book; by looking at things with fresh eyes, you too will find out just how easy it is to breathe new life into old spaces with verve and style in a matter of minutes or hours—not days. Who can resist the chance to think about their home in a new way and relish the thought that they're going to make it happen?

I've jam-packed *Style Solutions* with 365 ideas, one for every day of the year. All you have to do now is *go for it!*

Anne

living rooms

LEFT In this modern setting, the spotlight falls on the rough-hewn, asymmetric concrete lintel, appearing almost suspended in midair with a huge mirror behind. The opening, a discreet square, is painted white and hung with strands of large-scale amber and green beads, which are suspended from unseen cup hooks and glint in both sun and artificial light, mimicking the natural glow of real flames. A series of three abstract pictures, made inexpensively from gift wrap, hang at eye level in front of the mirror.

all fired up

Fires fascinate; going right back to our primeval roots, we're instinctively drawn to their warmth, glow, and ambience. Despite our modern heating systems, and even in hot climates, people continue to yearn for the special serenity and comfort that only real flickering flames can bring to a room. A fireplace will always attract attention, making a wonderful central feature around which the rest of a room can revolve. If blocked-up chimneys or other factors mean that your fireplace can't actually function, don't give up! Working or not, with a bit of imagination the fireplace can spark an entire room into life.

There's more than just the fire grate and the surround to consider—together with the hearth, mantelpiece, and wall space above they comprise one inviting canvas waiting to be decorated. The structure itself may be dramatic and imposing, or perhaps you wish to turn a stark, modern fireplace into one with a traditional look. Whether you've found yourself with an antique fireplace or a brand-new contemporary grate, there's lots of scope for exciting finishes, inventive display, and unexpected detail.

BELOW You can still have the glimmer of real flames in your living room if the fireplace doesn't work. A mass of twinkling tea lights spread in the opening creates a zone of luminosity and warmth, here almost shrinelike as they cast a glow on a reflective gold Thai statue. A circular mirror, surrounded by a band of mirror mosaics and positioned at the back of the fireplace, reflects and multiplies the shimmering light.

LEFT **With a little help, an unexciting pine surround freshened up with cream paint and contrasting dove gray in the recesses can provide real "wow" factor. Upholstery studs add an original and subtle detail (the position of each must be carefully measured and marked for a precise finish). The objects set out on the mantelpiece, including elegant, towering candles, a sumptuous flower arrangement, and a monumental sculpture, have been selected to add height, stature, and presence to the scene.**

tip

Keep a mantelpiece display fresh and vital by changing it every so often. Fresh flowers will naturally encourage you to vary the look, but reposition and rethink other items from time to time, experimenting with different pieces to create a variety of moods. Beware of letting a mantelpiece become cluttered—invitations, old postcards, and receipts can accumulate before you realize. Put them somewhere else and reserve the mantelpiece for well-chosen, beautiful objects that are rewarding to look at.

LEFT **A traditionally styled fireplace can be pepped up to suit young, modern tastes. See How to Make a Mosaic Tabletop on page 39 for instructions on creating this fragmented tile surface.**

tables

surface appeal

Living rooms should be lively and continually evolving—when was the last time you rearranged your living room furniture to give the space a fresh face without lifting a paintbrush or spending a cent? All too often, we get stuck in a rut, with a predictable, symmetrical arrangement of sofas and armchairs with a coffee table right in the middle. Sometimes large items are less flexible because of the constraints of your living room's proportions or layout, but a coffee table is generally small and light enough to be mobile. Take advantage! Experiment with varying locations for your table depending on whether you're relaxing alone with a cup of coffee and a magazine, serving drinks and nibbles to guests before a meal, or just watching TV with your partner.

If much of the furniture is arranged symmetrically, one out-of-kilter item will free up the whole setting. Rather than sticking to an established pattern, place your coffee table at an angle or slightly to one side instead of perfectly straight and centered, and feel things loosen up a bit.

how to make a blanket runner

Make a cozy-looking runner to brighten your coffee table on wintry days. This runner uses two throws: one a warm-toned plaid and the other a plain cream. The wooden table is dressed with a row of glass vases, each with an apple floating inside. It's a fresh, inviting look that you can easily put together at minimal cost.

1. Cut a strip from the checked throw approximately 12 inches in width, depending on the size of your table and how dominant you want the finished runner to be. Cut a strip from the contrasting plain throw, approximately 4 inches narrower, so it will lie centered on top with even margins of checked fabric showing on either side.

2. On the underside of the plain strip carefully measure and mark out a series of three equal squares, using a ballpoint pen or a marker. (Chalk won't show up sufficiently.) Use scissors to make a small hole in the center of each square, cut out toward each corner, then trim off the flaps to leave a clean square hole.

3. The throw will fray unless you seal and stabilize the edges of the squares to prevent them stretching out of shape. Use an iron-on bonding tape for a neat finish.

RIGHT This multipurpose occasional table also works as a storage unit for videos and CDs, and can be moved easily to one side after your coffee break. Made of painted wood, its no-frills removable lid provides a canvas for a decoupage tabletop. Decoupage can give a traditional or a very contemporary feel, depending on the layout, scale, and style of the pictures chosen. Here, photographs of flowers have been enlarged on a photocopier. Alternatively, try gift wrap or magazines for a useful source of images.

BELOW RIGHT A coffee table is part of your room's overall statement, and should be designed to add to the surroundings. The impact of multicolored stained floorboards is enhanced by a round coffee table segmented and stained in the same palette. The fun combination of stripes and circles, linked by color, is a showstopper. Masking tape, brushes, and wood stain or a colorwash are all it takes, but take the time to measure carefully and allow each painted section to dry before you peel off and reposition the tape for the next colored segment.

BELOW Mosaics are hard to beat in many locations in the home—so don't imagine they belong only in the kitchen or bathroom. A coffee table is just one more potential canvas. The hard surface is wipeable and if your living room contains mostly subdued tones, a mosaic coffee-table top can add a splash of vibrant pattern.

detailed cushions

BELOW **Use cushions to add a layer of detail that helps build the total scene, rather than act as a focus of attention themselves. Here, the delicate contrast of a velvet ribbon against a sheeny silk cover and the femininity of a dainty diamanté buckle trim impart pretty elegance.**

ABOVE **You can transform a store-bought cushion into a one-of-a-kind item by using an elaborate trim in a straightforward way. This pleated cushion in vibrant cerise is lifted out of the ordinary with an intricate but ready-made beaded braid. Lay and stitch at right angles to form an off-center cross.**

tip

It's difficult to carry colors and textures accurately in your head, so when you're shopping for finished cushions, or for fabric and trimmings to make your own, take swatches of materials, pieces of carpet, or other elements from your living room with you to minimize mistakes. Always keep receipts so you can return anything that looked perfect in the store but just doesn't work in your home.

just a trim

Cushions are the final accessories in a harmonious and inviting living space. The right choice of cushions can make or break the look of a sofa or armchair. Look at a variety of seductive fabrics, interesting finishes, and shapes and sizes that combine well together. It's useful to identify a color family—say browns, grays, and neutrals or blues and turquoises—and then choose a range of contrasting fabrics and embellishments from within your palette. Besides looking luscious and being irresistible to the touch, cushions have to be supportive and comfortable. Bear this in mind when you choose, make, or decorate cushions—hard beading or lumpy embroidery could be uncomfortable against your back or head.

BELOW LEFT AND BELOW **Go for an uncontrived look by mixing cushions in a plethora of textures and trims but within one family of tones. Velvet, silk, damask, embroidery, and beading in shades of cream, taupe, and chocolate are all combined here, contrasting nicely with a chestnut studded chair. A variety of sizes and shapes also gives a loose, natural feel.**

RIGHT **A little luxury can make an enormous difference. Plain oblong pillows are glamorized with long, glittery, beaded fringing, used only on the shorter sides. Although this beading can be expensive, the small quantity needed makes the project affordable.**

BELOW AND BELOW RIGHT **Use the same materials in different ways for coordinated variety. Embellished with beaded voile ribbon, one cushion has a single horizontal band, the other twin vertical bands at one end.**

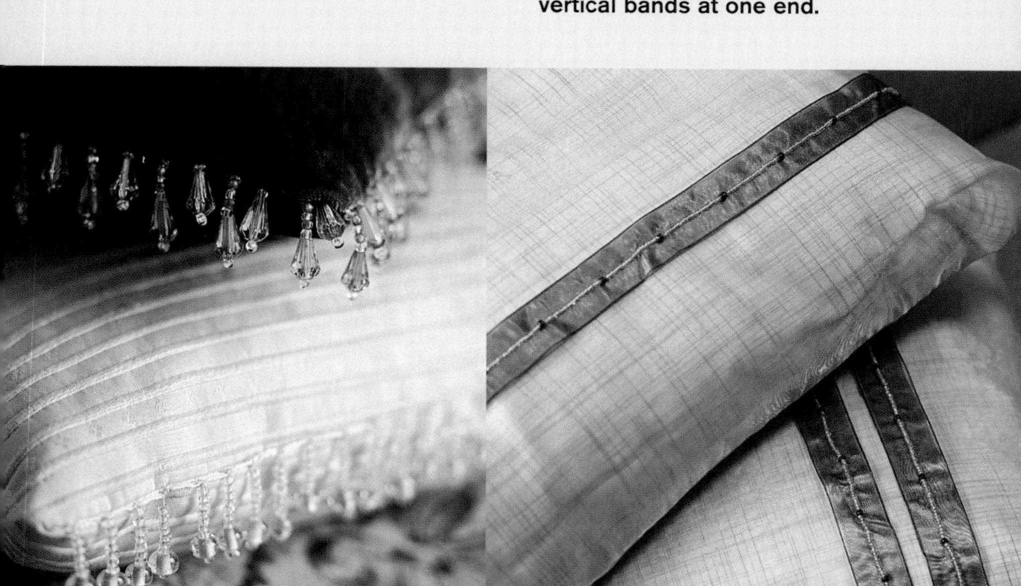

let there be light

Choosing the right lighting for a room is one of the trickiest decorating choices—you need flexibility for different tasks and times of day, and a variety of sources, from ceiling and wall lights to freestanding lamps. When you're shopping for lighting, you may be likely to concentrate on the type of base, be it wood, glass, metal, or china, that would suit your room and pay little attention to the shade. Lights very often come with a preselected shade, but think beyond whatever the shop has chosen for you. Lamp shades are as critical to the effect on your room as the base itself, and the right choice can really pull a look together. When the lamp is turned on, the shade must direct or diffuse the beam to suit your needs. During the day, lights are generally switched off, so a shade also has to pass the style test with the lamp switched both on and off.

ABOVE LEFT **The detailed surface of this lamp shade is the first thing you notice, despite the flamboyant wall decoration beyond. Large-scale blocks painted in browns and burnt oranges mirror the tones of a wood-grain-inspired fabric wrapped around the shade, but it is the complex effect of the shade that attracts the eye and puts the more dominant wall feature into perspective.**

CENTER LEFT **An etched design raises the profile of plain glass shades. The opaque pattern softens the glow from within and adds interest even when the light is off. Get creative with etching liquid and masking tape or stencils.**

LEFT **This store-bought lamp shade is a modern interpretation of a folkloric style. Its intricate embroidery, beading, hand-stitching, and sequined embellishments make it, rather than the base, the focus of the lamp. You might try incorporating different elements of the shade into combinations of your own.**

tip

A plain lamp shade in white or cream will allow any embellishment to stand out, and a regular, cylindrical shape is by far the easiest to decorate, lending itself well to measuring and wrapping. Before you glue anything permanently in place, lay the shade on the floor and add your trims, holding them in position with masking tape. Ribbons and fabrics will inevitably create a seam, so minimize an untidy effect by keeping all the seams in the same area on the shade, so this part can be turned to the back.

ABOVE RIGHT **An unadorned shade and some lengths of ribbon won't put much pressure on your wallet, but can add up to a luxuriant lamp shade. Best of all, this decoration takes very little planning. The design revolves around crystal-beaded ribbon, with bands of varying depths, and complementary tones as background.**

RIGHT **Naïve leaf shapes in sheer, delicate tones, wrapped in cream chiffon create the multilayered, almost fragile feel of this hand-decorated lamp shade. The chiffon leaves, a combination of four autumnal colors, use only a minimal amount of fabric. They have been treated with spray adhesive to hold them in place, then covered with a wrap of the same fabric in cream. Ribbon trim on the top and bottom finish the shade neatly. (Remember to line the seams up evenly together.) The layers of sheer fabric create a soft, subtle impression with the lamp either on or off.**

ottomans

LEFT AND BELOW **One ottoman can take on two quite different images with just a change of cover. A shimmery, tangerine satin cover, trimmed with a broad band of the same fabric in a sumptuous green shade makes this a glamorous spot to rest your feet for a snooze.**

BELOW RIGHT **A cotton print in a peacock-feather design gives a much more casual, homey feel. An ottoman can double as an occasional table for books or a tray of coffee, and if you add some generous pockets to the sides you'll always know where to find the remote control or your glasses.**

kicking back

Ottomans tend to be add-ons to your living room rather than part of the main "suite" of furniture. You might only decide to incorporate one after you've lived with your armchairs and sofas for a while and start to feel there's something missing—that vital, perfect place to rest your feet for maximum comfort while you read, watch TV, or doze. Rather than looking for another piece to match what you already have, take the opportunity to introduce a new fabric or color into your living room. Slipcovers are a brilliant way to keep the look of your ottoman fluid. They are simple to make and you can change them to create different moods, or alter the look of the room seasonally, adding warm, cozy woolens for winter and pretty florals for summer. Since most of us don't get to spend enough time with our feet up, when we do get the chance to be a couch potato, we might as well do it in style.

how to cover an ottoman

1. Measure the diameter of the top of the ottoman. Draw a circle on the fabric a bit larger than the top and cut out.
2. Measure the depth and length of the side panel/skirt. Cut fabric to size, again allowing extra fabric to attach the top and sides. Attach the panel/skirt to circle and slip on over the ottoman.

picture perfect

Pictures often work best in groups; a large collection of images, thoughtfully arranged over a substantial area, can add real drama to a living room. Even where space is limited, a detailed grouping has far greater impact than a solitary, lonely picture. The most trouble-free way to hang a selection of pictures is to opt for a symmetrical arrangement. Random groupings can look amazing but take quite a bit of skill, whereas you're guaranteed success with symmetry. It's helpful to lay the pictures out on the floor before you begin. Measure the dimensions of the complete group and stick a representative outline made from masking tape onto the wall to assess the size and effect. Meticulous measuring is paramount when you're putting up art. Whether you're hanging pictures or stenciling a design, to achieve the result you want spacing has to be perfect, so take your time.

ABOVE RIGHT **This array of photographs of tribal faces, backed by a charcoal-gray painted panel, is a very arresting display. As the focal point of a living room it might be overwhelming, but laid out on the wall connecting the living room to the kitchen, it brings unexpected interest to an otherwise bland space. The whole theme is played up by immense bamboo poles and a central, shield-shaped light fixture.**

CENTER RIGHT **Why buy a high-quality, high-priced frame to frame an expensive poster? This fragmented effect is inexpensive and easy to accomplish. The poster is pasted onto firm cardboard and then measured and cut into twelve equal squares. The wall is marked up, allowing regular gaps between the pieces. They are then mounted on the wall with Blu-Tack to form a jigsaw. The figures in the poster blend with the hazy, pink-toned colorwash on the wall behind to create the impression of an ancient, semi-uncovered fresco.**

RIGHT **A chimneybreast is an open invitation to hang something, but break away from the familiar, lone frame hanging exactly in the middle. A neat collection of six images has been carefully placed to look beautiful both up close and from a distance. The off-center layout is balanced by a tall vase filled with greenery on the hearth.**

tip

Be cautious when taking a hammer and nails or screws to your walls! Measure with great precision, marking spots with a tiny pencil dot. Check your measurements over again until you're absolutely certain that they are correct. Use a level to ensure that pencil dots are exactly level and horizontal. Make sure you also have some leftover paint or a piece of wallpaper so you can patch things up if you make a mistake or change your mind. Finally, use the level and Blu-Tack to ensure that the frames themselves are level.

ABOVE **A set of three identical framed pictures lends an unexpected twist to the space. Instead of being placed one directly below another, they are all at different distances from the side, but the gaps between them are exactly equal.**

LEFT **This large stencil design looks stunning against the yellow wall, but the key to its success is its position. Painted in the space behind the sofa, it is visually powerful but doesn't intrude when you're relaxing with your back to it. The most important aspect is the measuring and masking off of the squares to get the grid-pattern perfect. The gaps in between are simply the width of the masking tape. The color has been sponged on for a soft, mottled effect and stenciled with leaf-shapes.**

LEFT Using what is already in your home will help give your display a relaxed, personal feel. This serene grouping on a living-room ledge incorporates three brown-toned bottles and two small, rough-textured vases. A backdrop of three glass plates lets the soft pink of the wall behind come through. The plates, the only items specifically purchased for this display, have been enhanced with the addition of some copper leaf, used in a different format on each, so they make a loosely connected set. A trio of single, seasonal flower heads is the finishing touch.

BELOW RIGHT A small-scale display makes an enchanting foil for a dominant feature. Overlapping the edge of this imposing circular silver-leafed mirror above a fire-place, a hoop of magenta skeleton leaves echoes the ring shape but still lets you see the lustrous silvery frame behind. A row of four little tea lights supplies a subdued glow. The organic associations of the seasoned log and rich aubergine tone of the glass of the vase enhance the color and natural quality of the wreath.

stylish groupings

Before you rush out to shop for accessories to display in your living room, look around the rest of your home and check your cupboards and boxes to see what's already there. Take a step back and open your eyes to the possibilities of the many items you may have forgotten or never known how to use in your home. There may well be vases, bottles, carvings, stones, baskets, and any number of other objects in bedrooms, bathrooms, or kitchens that can be drawn together to make a complete picture. You'll also discover areas within your room whose display potential you might have overlooked, like a hearth, sideboard, or occasional table. Living-room displays should appear informal and unstudied, so it's well worth experimenting with pieces and learning by trial and error what pleases you.

ABOVE **Objects drawn from all corners of the globe can be brought together to create a display that hinges on texture and natural hues. Miniature woven baskets from Africa and flat, wide dishes with a burnished copper finish have been set against a cream-colored vase with a ribbed bowl on a dark wood sideboard.**

ABOVE **This array of glassware incorporates two colors, but the shapes are the real attraction. You probably won't find all the pieces for a finished grouping at the same time or in the same shop—be prepared to hunt and wait for exactly the right pieces. And be ready to buy when the correct item comes along—chances are you won't see it again.**

ABOVE **A hearth is a valuable display area that can help invigorate the fireplace all year round. This autumnal cluster takes only minutes to assemble and will last for several months. The centerpiece is a gleaming burnished-gold dish brimming with pinecones, cinnamon sticks, and dried lemon. Varying sizes of twig balls, bought from a florist, and a few extra cones have been allowed to stray onto the tiles and wooden floor.**

tip

To make a skeleton leaf wreath, buy a wire ring and predyed skeleton leaves from a florist or craft store. If you can only find natural ones, color your own with a fabric dye, testing first with a single leaf to get the right intensity. Find a suitable adhesive for use on metal, choosing an applicator with as fine a nozzle as possible, so you can apply tiny, neat dots of glue to the wire. Work your way around the wreath with glue and leaves as you go.

flowers

RIGHT **A couple of bunches of peach roses look like a million dollars in this glass cube vase. The display focuses on layers, moving from the inch-deep band of water at the base through bare stems, greenery, and finally the crown of rosebuds. The heads are positioned working from the sides inward. They are supported on a frame made from four twigs bound at the corners with sewing thread to form a square that rests on the vase. Cutting the stems to the correct length, stripping the leaves, and arranging the flowers in the frame all takes a little time, but it's well worthwhile for a special occasion display. Don't forget to replenish the water frequently!**

BELOW RIGHT **Flowers that blend in with their surroundings rather than stand out in a room deepen the complexity of the scheme, as they gradually become noticeable, rather than vying for attention. This natural, country-style arrangement in a gourd-shaped glass bowl is perfectly set off by the palette of blues and pinks that dominates the setting. Buy colored sand or gravel, more usually used in fish tanks, at pet shops to secure flimsy stems in your container. You can use the gravel again and again.**

tip

If you're going to use flowers regularly at home, it's well worth investing in a good-quality pair of pruning shears that will trim cleanly. Beware of cutting stems too short! To find the ideal length, place your vase on the edge of a table or worktop, then turn your flower upside down and hold the head just level with the tabletop. Check how high the stem extends above the top of the vase and mark with your finger where you want the flower head to sit. Cut with pruning shears, then turn the stem the right way up again—it should be exactly the right length.

petal power

Creating breathtaking floral arrangements can be quicker, cheaper, and far less stressful than you might imagine. Buying what is in season will always give you the very best value for your money—conversely, prices rocket if you insist on out-of-season species. Another good tip is to check out what's available in your local supermarket before stepping inside a florist shop—all the arrangements in this book were made with supermarket flowers. You'll often find an inexpensive and surprisingly varied selection. Just be prepared to be flexible about the selection, and you'll consistently spend much less than at a pricey florist. Go for a single type of bloom rather than mixed bunches, which can lack strength and authority.

Your vase plays as substantial a role in the total picture as the flowers. Clear glass is the ultimate in grace and versatility as it doesn't impose a color on the arrangement and gives you the freedom to exploit far more than just blooms. Placing stones, gravel, and even fruits in the water adds a whole new dimension to the bouquet. Use big containers with confidence. A small spray cleverly arranged in an oversized vase is a good change of pace from the typical cluster of flowers crowded into a small, insignificant container.

ABOVE LEFT **This minimalist arrangement turns your expectations upside down. Three dense bunches of bold, brushlike grass form a triangle. With the same proportion of stem below the rim of the vase as above, the whole display is perfectly balanced. Cut fruits look refreshingly natural floating in the vase.**

ABOVE CENTER **Three spectacular proteas backed by huge fan-shaped palm leaves create a personal paradise at home. The glass vase is virtually invisible, but some large stones placed in the bottom visually anchor the display to the table.**

ABOVE RIGHT **You can make a dynamic statement without a single petal in sight. This vibrant winter arrangement of berries, chilies, and evergreens has a fiery energy of its own. The sprays appear to be fighting for space with a mass of shiny, polished pebbles, then explode in a blaze from the top.**

framing the view

The way you dress a living room window influences the whole atmosphere of the room. Floral patterns, swags, and drapes bring an air of classic tradition; slim-slatted wooden venetian blinds feel cool and contemporary; and sheer, floaty voiles are the ultimate in softness and femininity.

Changing window treatments seasonally also helps create the right moods. Swap lightweight linens for warm wools and felts to transform your airy summer space into a snug cocoon for wintry nights. Window dressing falls into two categories: functional and nonfunctional. Some curtains, particularly full-length ones, can be just for show, framing the window with a blind behind for privacy. This trick allows you to indulge in an affordable amount of a luxurious fabric, as you'll need only enough material to dress the window, rather than sufficient to actually close the curtains properly.

ABOVE **A clever fabric combination can give an everyday window a modern twist. Here, two strikingly different materials—a lustrous voile in lime green, edged with lilac, and a plush, dusky blue velvet—have been hung together from parallel chrome poles. Clips hold the voile, while the front pole threads through extra-large metal eyelets along the top of the velvet. Matte and shiny surfaces in complementary tones are at the heart of this chic look.**

LEFT **A roller blind may be a budget option but it doesn't take much to make yours look special. Trimmings added to the bottom edge stand out nicely when the blind is partially lowered, since they fall in your sight line. You won't need much of any particular trim, so you can splurge a bit on a more complex series of textures and looks. With a glue gun, embroidered linen ribbon has been layered with a strip of ocher felt with a tiny, serrated edge. The final flourish is a length of mock-leather dressmaking fabric that doesn't fray, cut with scissors into exaggerated zigzags.**

LEFT Where a window lacks scale and grandeur, extravagantly trimmed curtains might be the answer. These professionally made botanical-pattern drapes with a fringed edge are purely decorative and are held open all the time. The focal feature of the sea-grass rope tiebacks are the oversized pinecones at the ends, which rest against the gathered fabric. The stalks of the cones have been bound together and the rope wound around the bases and secured with a glue gun.

how to make a leaf curtain

A fleece throw converts into a cozy, seasonal window dressing. The blanket is hung from a pole with no-fuss metal clips and decorated with simple, cutout leaf shapes in another shade of the same fabric.

1. Draw bold, simple leaf shapes onto paper and cut them out to make templates. Lay the throw out flat on the floor and pin the paper leaves on to work out the number and positions you want. Draw very faintly around each leaf, with chalk, then take each one off in turn, pin it to the alternative color of fleece, and cut it out.

2. Pin the leaves back in place, then sew them on with large, contrasting stitching through the center, to resemble the veins of the leaves. Finally, brush off any chalk and hang the curtain.

kitchens

freestanding cabinets

made to order

You'd expect to find a beautiful bureau or unique cabinet in the living or dining rooms, but when it comes to kitchens we tend to overlook the addition of beautiful furnishings. Somehow we think that kitchen furniture has to be fixed, fully fitted, and matching. Not so. Single items that break the mold stir up the whole room, giving you a chance to add character with an unexpected material, color, or shape. You could choose an armoire revamped as a store cupboard, or brightly painted, made-to-measure housing for your refrigerator-freezer. Conventional kitchen cupboards are more often than not designed to conceal. Certain items such as cleaning equipment are best kept out of sight, but not everything needs to be hidden. If you've got stunning glassware or an interesting assortment of crockery you want to show off, look for a piece that displays rather than screens its contents. Glazed, etched, or cutout doors, for example, let you have a sneak peek at what's inside. However you approach it, your kitchen will really benefit from a well-chosen freestanding item.

RIGHT **A thoughtfully designed piece is a feast for the eyes while making itself useful at the same time. This low-level cabinet that includes a work surface has a rounded shape, echoed in the dramatic, etched sweep across the curved glass front and the oversized circular handles. The glass, partially treated with etching paint, hides some objects while revealing others.**

LEFT **Freshly painted and fitted with new shelving, an old pine closet, as much at home in the kitchen as in the bedroom, becomes a focal feature. Branches from a pruning job were obtained from a local tree surgeon and turned into extraordinary door handles that add a natural and individual flavor. (Make sure they're dry and insect-free first.)**

RIGHT **A freestanding piece can be a mobile, multi-functional accessory that loosens the feel of a kitchen fitted with built-ins. Although this island has the same style as the rest of the room, it's set apart because it has a different work surface from the other units. Mounted on heavy-duty casters, it can easily move around wherever extra workspace is needed. One side also cleverly doubles as a neat breakfast bar.**

BELOW **Kitchen-related cutouts create a lively look on doors fitted on a bookcase, resulting in a smart, tall storage unit. Apart from the interesting patterns, cutouts let you see a hint of the contents and function as handles, too. If you live in an area where insects are a problem, place screening behind your cutouts. Try stencils for a variation on this look.**

BELOW **This large, red cabinet houses a washing machine and refrigerator-freezer. Its blue peaked roof has definition and presence of its own, ensuring that one corner of the kitchen dares to be different.**

BELOW **Outfitting cupboards for dry goods makes intelligent use of space in a long, narrow entrance to the kitchen, but solid doors would only emphasize how tight the passage is. Arc-shaped cutouts span the width of the unit, leading the eye into the room beyond and minimizing the sense of enclosure. The door handles are also cutouts, so nothing protrudes into the narrow access route.**

backsplashes

practically beautiful

Walk into any kitchen and one of the first things you'll notice is the backsplash. It's right in your line of vision and usually extends around a large section of the wall space. Being so prominent, it really is key to the overall look of a kitchen, but often gets less attention than it merits. If you opt for anything mundane, you're missing out on a brilliant opportunity to give a kick to your kitchen. Aside from conventional backsplash materials like tiles or stainless steel, other possibilities exist, such as painted wood, glass, granite, and slate. Although the appearance is important, you must balance style with practicality and be aware of the maintenance required by the different alternatives—stainless steel or mirrored surfaces look glorious but need frequent polishing to stay shiny; mosaic tiles are more forgiving.

ABOVE **Tiles are ideal for a backsplash, and the patterns, shapes, and colors available are limitless. For a spontaneous effect and a country flavor, pick plain tiles in three related shades and arrange them in a random way, interspersed with different embossed designs.**

ABOVE LEFT **A white-painted wooden backsplash sets the tone for a comfortable, farmhouse-style kitchen. Rather than leaving the top of the wood level, use a small saw to give each slat a point. You'll add interest to the kitchen by creating a panel evocative of a picket fence.**

ABOVE CENTER **Build up layers of texture and color for a practical backsplash that is visually both strong and subtle. Aluminum mesh against a painted wall lets the vivid blue show through, instantly drawing your eye. A sheet of glass on top ensures a protective, easy-to-care-for finish and adds depth and substance.**

tip

A backsplash can be added at almost any time, so explore all the possibilities and hone in on the overall look of the room. It's essential to see the material in position before you decide, so get good-sized samples to take home. Prop them against your kitchen wall so you can judge how the different options will look.

ABOVE **A minty aqua wall covered by a sheet of security glass with wire mesh makes a chic, effective backsplash that looks excellent alongside stainless steel utensils. The faint grid pattern adds an extra detail, mimicking tiny tiles.**

BELOW **This semicircular backsplash does service in a contemporary kitchen. Its bold shape, mirrored in the rounded, slate oven-surround and the subtle arc of the hood, makes it a focus. The arched design protects the wall as efficiently as a rectangle. When treated with a sealant after it has been fitted, slate is smooth, easy to clean, and won't absorb grease or stains.**

ABOVE **Where color is the essence of a kitchen design, there's no better choice than a laminated glass backsplash. Because it is transparent, it won't interrupt a strong scheme, and it has all the practical qualities you need. The scarlet wall behind the stove is almost seamlessly protected.**

ABOVE **Mosaic tiles are easy to apply and add detail and color to liven up any kitchen. Look for ready-made sheets of mixed patterns or design your own. These glass tiles have a bright, fresh quality perfect for a cheerful kitchen.**

BELOW **The vertical and horizontal lines of this fitted kitchen are reinforced in twin wall-mounted shelves and a slim steel backsplash and juxtaposed with sweeping painted curves and color contrast. Low-sheen acrylic paint makes for a water-resistant, wipe-clean finish, extending the backsplash well above the top of the steel.**

at hand

Containers are one of the crucial factors in keeping your kitchen looking polished and operating smoothly. Using containers for utensils or certain food items and keeping them out on view means there's more space behind cupboard doors for whatever you'd rather keep hidden, such as unattractive bottles of oils or sauces, a battered but favorite old pan, or your cleaning supplies. Containers allow you to have the items you need right on hand rather than shutting them away out of easy reach. They also help keep the kitchen tidy and your work areas clutter-free. Because they are on display, your containers have to measure up in looks as well as practicality, complementing the style and finish of appliances, gadgets, furniture, and flooring, so choose wisely, and have some fun!

ABOVE LEFT AND LEFT **There are a profusion of standard wine racks available, but for a real original, why not ask a carpenter to build something special, or even tackle the task yourself? Made from two circles of wood with holes for the bottles to slot in, then painted, this rack is an incredibly simple construction that looks sensational on a wall or countertop and holds a generous collection of bottles.**

RIGHT **With their myriad tones and textures, spices are worth displaying. A spice rack on runners, filled with rows of identical clear glass jars, can be pulled out when you need it, and pushed back neatly afterward.**

BELOW Cut fresh herbs last only a few days, so they have to be used quickly and replenished often. Why not buy potted herbs and place the pots in stout, little aluminum buckets on the windowsill or counter? Water them every couple of days, allow them to get some sunlight, and they'll not only look charming but give you plenty of cooking inspiration. If you do buy cut herbs, you can also fill the buckets with water and submerge the stems to keep them from wilting.

how to wrap a pot

A terra-cotta pot costs just a few dollars, but embellish it with rope and it makes a superb, rustic kitchen container. A roomy pot is perfect for bigger tools like rolling pins or whisks.

1. Choose a length of thin, flexible natural rope with a rough texture. Pick a pot in the size you need. Using a glue gun, start at the top of the pot, just under the rim, to secure the first inch of your rope, pointing down to the base.

2. Push the length of rope up, press it firmly under the lip, and start coiling it around the pot, covering the starting place. Keep winding around and down the pot, compressing the strands of rope every few rows, to hide the terra-cotta completely.

3. At the bottom, glue the end of the rope firmly in place and trim if necessary.

have a seat

Tables and chairs are usually freestanding pieces in the kitchen, rather than part of any built-in furniture or workspace. Because they are one of the largest pieces in a kitchen, tables in particular will make a big statement, so choosing the right piece is vital. An unappealing or uninteresting choice could affect the entire look of the room.

These days, the kitchen table needs to be multifunctional. Meals may involve two people one day and ten the next. It's probably also where the kids do their art projects and where parents compile shopping lists, make cookies, and do paperwork. Seek out flexible furniture with such elements as adjustable height and extending or folding sections to meet your requirements.

Chairs, too, are worth thinking about carefully. Stools are fine if you only ever stop for a quick drink, but for all the other activities, including meals, you need chairs that are the correct height, supportive, and comfortable to sit on for any length of time.

ABOVE RIGHT **Folding chairs are convenient for flexible seating, but they can be pretty onerous to sit on for long. Add a loose cushion to pad either the back or the seat as necessary. For a dash of wit, convert a classic-style tea towel into an inexpensive cushion.**

RIGHT **The most basic wooden table can readily take center stage in the kitchen with the help of some paint and a large-scale stencil. Here, the tabletop has been colorwashed in a pale blue, then a leaf stencil applied. The leaves have a soft, uneven finish and are scattered in a way that feels natural and unplanned. Two coats of acrylic varnish guarantee a quick-drying, hard-wearing, wipe-clean top.**

LEFT Out-of-the-ordinary seating combinations are an effortless way to add panache to your kitchen table. Try flea markets for inexpensive mismatching chairs that can be painted different colors for an irreverent, unstudied look. Here, budget plastic chairs are used for everyday, but when more room is required, the table can be pulled away from the side so that nifty wall-mounted seating can slide down smoothly into position. The mixture of intricately crafted natural wooden seats and white plastic is quirky and unexpected.

BELOW LEFT A table suspended from steel tension wires makes a dramatic focus in a modern kitchen setting.

how to make a mosaic tabletop

The mosaic-covered top is made from marine ply and smashed ceramic tiles. This is quite a labor-intensive project—a tabletop could take a day or longer to finish, depending on its size—but the unique and long-lasting results make it well worth the effort.

1. Wear goggles to protect your eyes. Put your tiles all together in an old pillowcase or cloth bag and smash them with a hammer.
2. Tile in sections, starting at one edge and working toward the center. Spread tile adhesive toward the middle, then begin to add tile, mixing sizes for an irregular appearance. Continue tiling around the edge and inward until the whole circumference is completed. Work in small sections to fill in the center.
3. When finished, allow 24 hours for the adhesive to set. Grout the tiles, using a contrasting white grout. Wipe off the residue with a damp cloth and allow to dry.

tabletops

casual settings

The kitchen is a place for minimum-effort table settings. Save fancy flower arrangements and elaborate centerpieces for the dining room and stick to witty, lighthearted touches that you can put together quickly to create a comfortable, casual ambience. Look to incorporate items that you use regularly in the kitchen as part of the display—tablecloths, napkins, place mats, and so on—and just present them in a more thoughtful way, costing next to nothing in cash or time, but making them much prettier to look at.

tip

Fabric paints are ideal for pepping up plain fabrics like napkins and tablecloths, and you can use them either freehand or with stencils. For the best results, choose a closely woven cloth, which will act as a firm surface for the paint, rather than a very open weave, and allow each color to dry properly before you add the next.

LEFT **Stenciled words around the hem of a tablecloth elevate it above the norm. Use food-related words and phrases—"delicious," "yummy," "scrumptious," or "bon appétit"—the names of meals, days of the week, or even something like "It's the weekend!"**

ABOVE RIGHT **With a pot of chalk nearby, a child's blackboard is a ready-made place mat that offers a place for kids and grown-ups to scribble in between courses—excellent for keeping kids occupied at the table.**

RIGHT **A baking tin that doesn't get a great deal of use in the oven can have a second life as a planter. Filled with tiny alpines and topped with shale, it will bring a hint of vitality to the table for many weeks and require very little maintenance.**

display

LEFT **Kitchen equipment should be worth showing off. Of course, it has to be functional, but as you build up a collection of appliances and utensils, go for styles, colors, and materials that form a picture, rather than miscellaneous bits that don't have anything in common. Choose a toaster, coffee maker and dishrack that blend comfortably with the tones and textures around them. Stick only to stainless steel bakeware and you can hang it in a gleaming cluster on a wall, freeing up cupboard space.**

CENTER LEFT **Whatever the climate, you can use your window to bring something of the outside into your kitchen. An etched semicircle on the lower half of the glass disguises a dull, square pane and focuses the eye, directing you to the garden vista beyond.**

on show

The kitchen is probably called on to perform more functions than any other room in your home. Apart from being used to prepare and enjoy meals and clean up afterward, it might be the room for letter writing, household repairs, homework, or craft projects. It's probably also the social center where family and friends gather informally to snack and chat. Choosing what to display in the kitchen is all about creating the right atmosphere for these different activities. The items on show may well be food- or cooking-related, but they should still please the eye or make you smile. The coffeepot or toaster you select, and even your aprons and dish towels and the way they are placed, contribute to the impression. Don't strive for the clinical character of a state-of-the-art restaurant kitchen—above all a kitchen should feel homey, welcoming, and relaxed, and the right displays will help you achieve this.

ABOVE **The word *Cuisine,* made from painted wooden letters and glued to a beam above the cupboards, fills a gap with ease but not clutter, giving out a sociable, laid-back vibe.**

ABOVE RIGHT **An empty pane above French doors can be turned into a surprising place for a low-key display. Etching liquid has been used with stencils depicting kitchen utensils and a sprinkling of cooking words to produce a whimsical alternative to plain glass.**

BOTTOM LEFT AND RIGHT **In a working kitchen you need a whole range of articles at your fingertips, from herbs and spices to utensils and gadgets. The ones you use most frequently should be at the ready, so you're not constantly having to search for them. Shelves solve the problem, but it's not only about what goes on them. Pay attention to how they look, taking the opportunity to introduce detail in their style.**

eye-catching

Function is often the priority when you are outfitting your kitchen. You do need appliances that work well, practical surfaces, and an efficient layout, but since you and and your family are likely to spend a substantial amount of time in this room, it also must seem friendly, welcoming, and personal. Details are the key. They are usually touches that are strictly nonessential, either minor add-ons, like pictures and plants, or larger features, integral to the design, such as the color scheme. Details are worth special consideration because they'll transform the space from a utility area into a room with personality and charm.

how to make a 3-D collage

1. This 3-D image is a smart way to enliven a blank wall above a shelf or workspace. Buy an inexpensive, narrow wood picture frame, hold it against the wall, and mark the inside corners with a pencil dot. Draw lines with a ruler to join the corners to form a rectangle. Mask the edges of the shape with masking tape, then paint it blue.

2. Paint a selection of wooden kitchen utensils in the same color. Use spoons, spatulas, and whisks in as wide a selection of shapes and sizes as you want. Paint the frame as well.

3. When dry, use a glue gun to fix the utensils to the painted area of the wall in a haphazard, overlapping way, as if they'd been thrown there. Finally, remove the masking tape and attach the frame around the background.

LEFT Plants are a cheerful, life-affirming addition to any room. Choose low-maintenance, evergreen species like cacti or succulents for the kitchen. Place a potted plant in a colander and fill the space around it with gravel for a whimsical, unexpected take on the usual houseplant.

ABOVE Floors, one of the largest areas in a room, can give you a huge canvas for a real statement. Wood is an excellent, practical choice for kitchens, but you needn't limit yourself to just one shade. Here, plywood squares have been treated like floor tiles. Stained with a whole spectrum of related shades and laid in a random checkerboard pattern, this flooring is going to be noticed.

RIGHT No kitchen is complete without cupboards, but they don't have to match each other exactly to do the job. Contrasting colors and style variations in the doors and fittings will keep things fresh and punchy. A vivid blue door can sit happily beside a peach one with a large etched panel. The shelves below double as both storage and a display area.

ABOVE Although it might be kept in the kitchen, a drawer unit is handy for storing all sorts of bits and pieces that are not strictly kitchen related. It may hold craft materials, seed packets, letters and notepads, pet care paraphernalia, sewing equipment, or small tools. Make it blend in by giving it a foody flavor, even if there's nothing to eat inside! Give freehand painting a shot, or photocopy an attractive label for a template to guide you.

ABOVE In just a few minutes, with a small amount of cash, you can give a bare wall a splash of vibrant color and a food-related theme. Find a kitchen-friendly image you like—it could be from a postcard or an old cookbook or magazine. Place it in an inexpensive pine frame and use gleaming brass pins to attach dried bay leaves all around the edge. The result is bright and fresh.

bedrooms

pampering touches

When you think about what you want from your bedroom, put comfort right at the top of the list. Any other functions you expect your bedroom to serve should come second as you plan the place you will retreat to at the end of the day to switch off, put up your feet, and pamper yourself. Comfort stems both from small visual touches like a bowl of flowers and larger, textural features such as a fabulous cushioned headboard. When you enter your bedroom it should feel like a warm sanctuary filled with soft, welcoming fabrics, pleasing sights, and gentle scents, all helping you forget life's pressures for a while.

BELOW **Many pets love to follow their owners wherever they go, including the bedroom. Outfit a basket or choose cushions in coordinating colors to give your best friend her own exclusive nighttime comfort zone. Make sure it's at least as blissful as yours, or they'll only try to muscle in on your bed.**

BELOW **A hot-water bottle is the ultimate comforting cuddle. Make a soft felt bottle jacket just for this purpose, add a drawstring top, and label it with big, clear cutout felt letters, fixed with iron-on adhesive backing. What better way to keep your toes cozy on a chilly night?**

FAR LEFT **The smallest bedroom can be huge on comfort. This tiny room makes clever use of space, with concealed under-bed storage, but its most striking feature is a full wall of luscious, purple-silk padding, reminiscent of an oversized headboard. The padding envelops the space with almost womblike softness and, coupled with glowing silk bedding, creates an irresistible hideaway.**

BELOW **An arrangement of flowers and candles enhances the tranquil atmosphere of a bedroom both during the day and through the evening. Four dampened strips of florist's oasis wedge a candle into the center of this square bowl, leaving a gap all around for flowers. With the stems trimmed short, the heads, a mixture of miniature and large-scale blooms in white and yellow, rest level with or just above the rim of the bowl. Stick the stems in the moist oasis so they will stay fresh for several days. Flowers for day, candles by night.**

tip

When a man and woman share a room, it's important for each to feel totally at home with its decor. An overly feminine scheme, all floral prints and frills, could make him feel uncomfortable, whereas she might not enjoy the sober colors or graphic checks and stripes that are traditionally more masculine in tone. Try to achieve a balance in the choice of colors, fabric, and furniture so that both partners have an environment in which they can take things easy.

BELOW **If you enjoy using scents as part of your unwinding routine, make your own aromatherapy center on a tray that you can bring out in the evening. Drill a row of five holes along the top of a small log and push an incense stick into each one. Set the log on a flat dish and surround it with dried lavender. Arrange the dish on the tray with your oils, light the incense sticks, and relax.**

bedding

lap of luxury

Bed linens tend to follow fashion trends and seasons, so you'll notice similar palettes, materials, textures, and details appearing in both apparel and homeware departments at certain times of the year. If you're looking for something with a hint of originality, or to fit into your particular bedroom scheme, buying plain bedding and making it special yourself could be the best move. Small trims and touches are all you need, so tailoring bed linens to your look shouldn't be complicated, costly, or demanding.

BELOW **You can't beat luxurious fabrics for making a really cozy, inviting bed for winter nights. Use rich velvets in strong colors for a statement headboard mixed with two-tone velvet pillows, or combine a refined white bedcover with a pale blue faux fur throw.**

ABOVE **Beribboned pillowcases can single-handedly dress up and personalize a bed. Have two or three pillows just for show, embellish them with a crisp mix of plain and detailed bows and trims, and stack them on the bed, leaving a plain one at the bottom for actually sleeping on. Check washability before you buy and don't attach your ribbons until you've washed them and the pillowcases at least once. "Dry clean only" ribbons won't be suitable for everyday pillowcases.**

how to stamp linens

A rubber stamp, a small roller, and some fabric paints will convert boring plain sheets and pillowcases into pretty prints. The method is easy, but work slowly and precisely for a clean, expert result. For smaller designs, rubber stamps perform better than stencils, producing a finer, more intricate image that doesn't overload the cloth with fabric paint.

1. Pick a stamp and two shades of fabric paint. Working on a spacious bench or table, lay out a generous sheet of kitchen foil. Pour a small line of paint onto the foil and draw it down with your roller. Roll a little paint onto the stamp, taking great care not to glop it on or you will lose clarity in the stamp. Then test for the color and effect, ideally on a spare piece of the linen you're planning to decorate; you can also use an old rag. (It's a good idea if possible to buy an extra pillowcase as a tester when you're buying new bedding for stamping.) Check the resulting tone, as colored fabric will affect the appearance, and practice stamping carefully to achieve the best definition you can.

2. Whether you're decorating brand-new or older linen, it should be washed and ironed as smooth as possible before you start. When you're ready to begin, tape the item flat on the table with masking tape. If you're working on a sheet, place a piece of foil underneath. If it's a pillowcase or duvet cover, slip a piece of foil inside—this adds stability and prevents paint from seeping through onto the back of the pillowcase or other fabric beneath. If you choose a repetitive pattern, mark it out with small pieces of masking tape to guide you. Remember to wash and dry the stamp and roller thoroughly when changing colors.

bed canopies

how to create a four-poster look

You don't need a bed with posts to give the illusion of an elegant four-poster. This treatment uses lengths of inexpensive, lustrous material to softly swathe a pine bed.

1. Bore a small hole in the ceiling, above and a few inches out from each corner of the bed. This will allow the fabric to hang clear of the mattress. The holes must be large enough to hold a wall anchor securely. Use a hammer and screwdriver to tap a wall anchor into each hole, then choose a cup hook of a suitable size and screw it into the hole as far as it will comfortably go.

2. Hang a curtain ring from each hook. The size of ring depends on the bulk of the fabric you want to suspend. Use string to gauge the amount of material you need, attaching a length of string to one ring, then draping it across to the next, and so on, making a rectangle. The string should dip a little between the corner points—if the fabric is too taut the luxurious effect will be lost. When the tension is right, take down the string, measure it, and add a little extra to allow for fastening to the rings. Use string again to work out the fabric needed from the ceiling to the floor, including excess to drape on the floor.

3. Knot the drapes to the rings. You may find it easier to complete the top section first, followed by the vertical lengths, and to divide your cloth into eight sections. There should be two longer and two shorter pieces for the top and four identical pieces to hang from the corners to the floor.

tip

Be generous with your material! If it is pulled too tightly around the top, your canopy will lose its deluxe feel. Likewise allow plenty of length at each corner—for a truly opulent feel, the cloth should fall in extravagant fabric pools on the floor.

illusions of grandeur

A canopy gives a bedroom a real sense of drama. You might associate a four-poster look with the rooms in a top-class hotel or a luxurious home, but you can create the same look without difficulty. You don't need a huge space, a special kind of bed, unlimited cash, or even professional help. A basic bed can be dressed and draped surprisingly easily, using hooks, poles, and lengths of fabric. There are many options that can take less than a day to assemble, and can be easily removed or changed when you wish.

tip

In a smaller room, lightweight choices (like netting and voiles, which don't visually overwhelm space) will work best. A bed canopy may not be the right move in an extremely low-ceilinged room, where it could just emphasize the lack of height. In this case, look at ways of focusing attention on the headboard, perhaps with drapes, an exaggerated scale and shape, or a distinctive decorative treatment.

how to make a draped canopy

The black-and-white canopy is what you notice in this unusual bedroom. The bed itself is very plainly dressed, and the bold graphic stripes—balanced by the diamond-painted screen to one side and a whimsical papier-mâché Great Dane dog to the other—immediately grab your attention. This canopy consists of a pair of curtain poles, suspended from the ceiling by chains held on cup hooks, over which a length of fabric is draped.

1. **First put the poles up. They hang directly over the head and foot of the bed, but the height of the room will determine how far below the ceiling they should be—you'll have a larger gap with a higher ceiling. Put cup hooks into the ceiling at each corner (see step 1, opposite), hook on the first and last links of a length of chain to form a loop, and suspend the poles horizontally.**
2. **Attach a length of string to each end of one pole and run the two strings in parallel to meet the other pole. This will show how the actual fabric will curve and give you the finished length required. Add on enough to allow for hems, a slot at either end into which the poles slide, and decorative front and back panels too, if you wish. Add your choice of finish, such as a zigzagged edge with tassels, fringing, or a contrast band.**

bedside and dressing tables

a touch of class

Your bedroom should be a haven of comfort, and not just the physical comfort provided by your mattress and pillows. Making do by piling random things on the floor by the bed or balancing a mirror on your knee to apply makeup isn't what you deserve. A bedside table is essential for your lamp, clock, book, glasses, or a drink. For cosmetics, hairbrushes, lotions, and perfume, a dressing table with a well-angled and generous mirror for applying makeup and styling your hair is a must. You can adapt existing items or spruce up uninteresting, off-the-shelf numbers to blend them in with the ambience of the room.

BELOW **These clear mock crystal drawer pulls look stunning set against the mirrored panels. The woodwork is painted a soft green that complements rather than detracts from the glass. Pearl and glass accessories play up the chic nostalgia of this unmistakably feminine dressing table.**

ABOVE LEFT **Color and decoration in keeping with the muted, chalky palette of the room can bring a young, fresh feel to a pair of plain bedside tables. A pale lime-green colorwash with a faint cross-hatch grid pattern, stenciled with leaf silhouettes in gentle pastels, makes the perfect backdrop for a gracefully wrought lamp and fresh flowers.**

ABOVE CENTER **Anything flat can be displayed underneath a topping of plain glass—try photographs, paintings, cutout letters, dried leaves, lace, fabrics, and even notes or stamps. This painted dressing table was undistinguished until lipstick-red fake rose petals scattered within a painted border brought it into a new dimension. Try different flowers for different moods.**

LEFT **This pine piece, transformed by mirrored glass, could have graced a starlet's dressing room in the glamour days of Hollywood. Measure the top and the drawer fronts accurately. Ask a glazier to cut the mirrors and polish the edges smooth. Give him the existing handles to show the size and position of the holes to be drilled in the glass for them. Lay the top sheet on the table. Stand the drawers on end and glue the mirrored fronts on, using a special glass adhesive available from your glazier. When the glass is set, replace the handles with crystal-look acrylic ones.**

tip

A dressing table needs a tough, easy-to-clean surface that can stand up to hairspray, powder, creams, and makeup, as well as hard items like metal containers and plastic combs. Wood and paint can be easily scratched and marked, but a glass top is the solution. It will protect a more delicate surface below, wipes clean, and looks wonderful.

detail

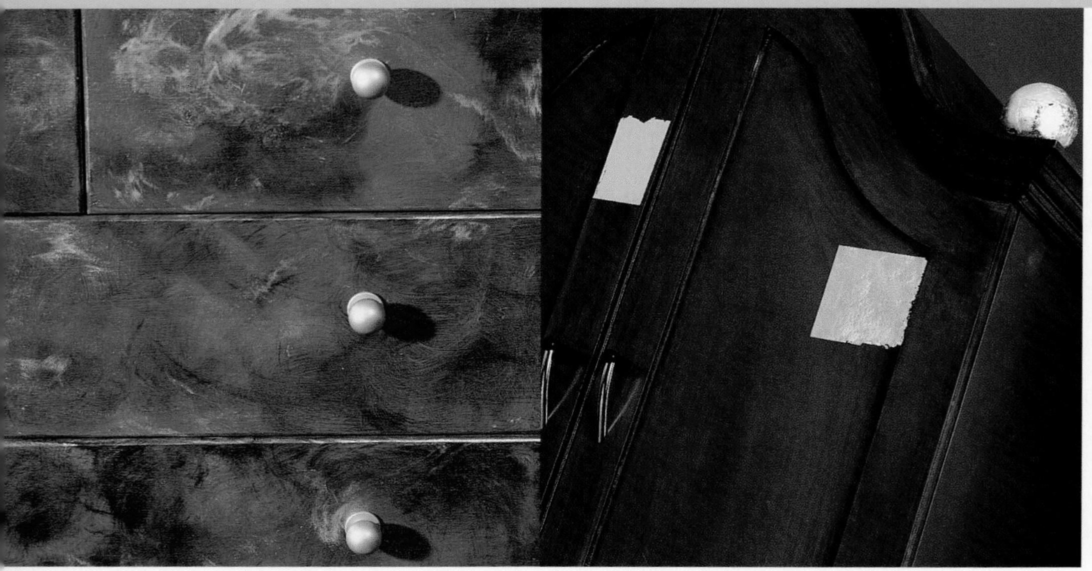

LEFT **Antique-style furniture can be successfully updated with contemporary detail. Here, silver-leaf squares placed at random on the front give this classic closet a modern twist, and underscore the carved features. Discreet contemporary chrome handles complete the "old meets new" mix.**

ABOVE **Well-chosen fittings and a special finish, such as a paint effect, can revive old or inexpensive furniture. Three shades of blue and a dusting of silver to blend with the tiny painted handles elevate a mundane pine chest to something wonderful.**

BELOW LEFT **Sets of silk lavender-filled pillows of different tones, stacked and tied with contrasting ribbon, will delight the eye, where a single one would hardly be noticed. These take no time to put together and add a hint of scent and style, tucked among lingerie, bed linens, towels, or in a shoe drawer.**

BELOW **Some items, like these charming embroidered slippers, are just too perfect to wear or to shut away in a cupboard. Suspended on a generous length of satin ribbon and hung from a closet door, they have a chance to show off their elaborate handiwork and make a unique display. Stuff the toes with potpourri for a hint of fragrance.**

finishing touches

Details can add charm, and perhaps a sprinkling of intrigue, to your sanctuary. They may be tiny, exquisite items, chosen solely for their beauty, or larger pieces like thoughtfully finished furniture. They should blend with the room's decor rather than fight for your attention and have a natural, uncontrived feel, as if they are there almost by chance. Don't race to hide away all of your belongings—take a moment to pick out some of your prettiest items and think of ways to show them off. And take a closer look at the larger pieces of furniture in the room. Sometimes a little embellishment is all that is needed to transform them from merely functional to fantastic.

RIGHT **The fragile cherry blossom is the most romantic of flowers and, combined with a string of pearl beads in a glass vase, makes an elegant display for a bedside table. Buy a fake-pearl necklace to hold the blossoms in place and allow them to spill naturally over the side of the vase. Through the glass you can clearly see the beads winding around the branch below the water.**

intimate dressing

Bedroom window treatments should provide privacy at night and help you wake up comfortably each morning. Some of us love opening our eyes to a room flooded with daylight, and for those people, pale curtains are fine. If you're not a morning person and prefer to drift gently toward consciousness in dimmer light, choose darker-toned curtains or blinds that will block or at least diffuse strong early sunshine. A window with a built-in heater below can be awkward to dress. Full-length curtains help give a bedroom that essential indulgence factor, but they will block some of the heat, while sill-length styles are high on practicality but low on luxury. A good compromise is to fit blinds for privacy and to block light and hang full-length curtains to frame and define the window. This will give you the sumptuous visual effect you want without covering the heat source.

ABOVE LEFT **Transform an everyday woven roller blind into a picture of femininity just by pushing fake flowers through the fabric to create an informal, delicate scattering. Fix the heads with masking tape until you're happy with the spread and blend of tones, then secure them to the blind with glue. You may only be able to decorate the bottom third of the blind, avoiding the area to be rolled up so as not to crush the flower heads. Voile curtains on either side soften the window edges.**

ABOVE **The plainest white cotton curtains bring an airy feeling to a bedroom, yet can have detail and interest in themselves and won't break the bank. Here, strips of contrasting indigo-blue ribbon have been added for a classic, fresh blue-and-white combo. Ribbons are attached discreetly every couple of inches along the top edges, then left to hang loose. Cut to various lengths, some reach only about a third of the way down; others are almost at the floor. The ribbons form irregular stripes when the curtains are closed and bunch together when they're open.**

LEFT Very tall windows can be expensive to dress, and if yours are exceptionally tall, you may have difficulty finding ready-made curtains to fit. The solution is to buy inexpensive curtains and customize them by adding a plush bottom border to extend the length. It's important to choose an add-on cloth of a similar weight to the existing material and to achieve as sharp a finish as you can. A deep border of textured material in a rich shade of eggplant added to very inexpensive yellow curtains gives them the look of a far more extravagant purchase.

BELOW The main heat source of this room is under a large bay window, yet full-length curtains can still be hung to make the most of the graceful trio of windows. Neat blinds, pulled down with smart tassels, give flexibility for privacy or daylight as required. Tasteful cream curtains bordered by a wide band of green fabric can either hang naturally at the sides or be gathered with tiebacks, but are never actually drawn across the window.

storage

a place for everything

Bedrooms have important storage roles to play. When you're not relaxing and resting, you might be busy dressing, styling your hair, making small repairs, or putting away clothes, bags, and shoes. You'll want to have a number of items on hand for your bedroom rituals—your room won't function efficiently if absolutely everything is behind doors or tucked out of sight in drawers and boxes. Storage can be part of the display and character of the room, whether in the form of a customized and eye-catching closet or a bowl of pretty cosmetics on a dressing table.

how to label a shoe bag

1. Photograph your pair of shoes using a normal camera. Take the picture in good light, ensuring the items fill the frame. Enlarge the photograph on a photocopier to the right size to fit on the front of the bag and cut it out.

2. Use either a fabric transfer liquid or fabric transfer paper, available from craft shops, to reproduce the image on the fabric bag. Follow the directions on the packaging—some products give a gloss finish and others a matte result.

Protect your most treasured shoes in soft shoe bags. A photographic transfer on the outside means you'll know right away which bag you want. The same principle would also save you time by identifying opaque garment bags if you have several coats, dresses, or suits stored together.

RIGHT **An uninteresting run of closets can become the star attraction if you simply rethink the conventional approach to doors. Cut in interlocking curves rather than straight lines, these doors make a design statement, reinforced by unusual, randomly placed handles.**

BELOW **There's no need to hide away attractive objects like hair accessories. Laid on a circular glass cake stand they make an engaging feature on a dressing table.**

BELOW RIGHT **A bedroom drawer is a useful spot for keeping sewing materials at your fingertips for speedy repairs like fixing a loose button or hem. Keep all the small bits and pieces in order with a few dishes and baskets placed in the drawer to separate threads, beads, needles, and scissors for easy access.**

bathrooms

paint effects

LEFT Geometric detail squares of white punctuate a vibrant blue background. Clean, uncomplicated lines make a splendid statement for any bathroom, especially smaller ones.

BELOW LEFT Vertical stripes of varying widths in tangerine, dusky gray, aubergine, and soft lime add dimension to a plain bathroom wall and highlight the rich plum paneled area.

BELOW The soft-sheen midnight blue color works well when complemented by the tall, slim gilt-trimmed mirror, offset by the pairs of pictures in matte blue frames and the dried moss-ball topiaries.

brush with success

If irresistible faucets or a magnificent floor have swallowed up most of your bathroom budget, you might be left wondering how to make the walls measure up without spending too much more. Tile throughout is a fabulous look, but could add to the dent in your finances. Paint is the solution, an inexpensive and potent tool. Today limitless colors and a plethora of finishes are available. Paint can be a breathtaking alternative to tiling. You need little more than an ordinary paint brush and a gutsy attitude to produce some evocative effects and to give your bathroom a bit of pampering, turning it into a lavish comfort zone.

tip

A strong, symmetrical statement gives the whole sink area real presence. Accessorize thoughtfully, flanking the sink with matching pairs of chunky candles, original pictures, contrasting vases, or decorative bottles and position an anchoring item, such as a mirror, in the center to properly focus even the smallest bathroom.

how to brush behind the sink

1. **Use bronze metallic paint as a base for a striking lattice design. To create a textured finish, use irregular brush-strokes first, then finish with strokes in one direction.**

2. **Use latex paint to make random vertical and horizontal dashes across the wall. Slowly lift the brush from the wall as you reach the end of each stroke, for a perfect effect.**

3. **Allow the first color to dry, then repeat with the second and third colors.**

how to create a backsplash

1. With a ruler and pencil, draw your design on the back of the sheet and cut it out with scissors. Remember to draw your design in reverse.

2. Check that your design is correct before you affix the tiles to the wall.

3. Apply the adhesive directly to the tiles to prevent it from getting onto parts of the wall that will not be covered with mosaic.

versa-tile

Mosaics have been around for centuries. The ancient Romans used them extensively, creating many stunning designs that can add interest to bathrooms in the twenty-first century. Mosaics look complicated, but they're actually relatively easy to execute. Today, glass mosaic tiles come stuck to a sheet of paper or mesh backing for easy application and the simple creation of geometric designs. You needn't detach individual tiles—simply cut the shape you want with scissors, stick it on, and peel off the paper. Plus, mosaics can be applied to any rounded surface, from a small vase to the side of a huge, curved bathtub. You can also cut out and insert strips, patches, or even single tiles of different colors to let your creativity shine.

tip

Don't leave your tile grout to harden for too long before you wipe it off. Unlike smooth ceramic tiles, glass mosaic tiles have an uneven surface, which adds to their charm. After the grout partially hardens, use a moist sponge to wipe down the mosaic, regularly rinsing the sponge as you go. Buff with a dry cloth.

4. Arrange the tiles on the wall, press gently and evenly, and leave them to dry for twenty-four hours.
5. Use a wet sponge to dampen the backing sheet, then peel it away from the tiles.
6. Sponge on the grout, wiping off excess with a second damp sponge. Allow it to partially harden and clean off thoroughly. Buff with a dry cloth.

privacy, please

Dressing a bathroom window provides an ideal opportunity to make a statement. Bathrooms benefit from good ventilation and as much natural light as possible for tasks like applying make-up, painting toenails, or shaving. Privacy is another vital consideration, and while you don't want to obscure the light, you also don't wish for the neighbors to oversee your daily rituals. Bathroom windows have to be multifunctional, allowing light and fresh air to enter while preserving your modesty. It is actually because of these competing needs that some stylish windows have been manufactured to offer attractive diffused light and intricate detailing while preventing a clear view of the room.

ABOVE **For a modern, edgy take on stained glass, cut colored adhesive film into uncomplicated shapes and stick them carefully to a windowpane, one color at a time, smoothing out any air bubbles with a ruler's edge as you go..**

BELOW **Handcrafted stained glass may have a hefty price tag, but you can create your own stained effect using a glass-painting kit and a dramatic stencil. A clear, simple design and a powerful, punchy color will achieve the most striking results.**

tip

For a crisp contrast, costume jewelry and a few stitches have transformed a boring blind with a tasteful and charming trim.

TOP LEFT AND ABOVE **Bathrooms don't always have striking window frames. Hide a less than lovely one behind stylish opaque glass frames. The glass was etched in white and green, for the perfect combination of privacy, light, and decoration.**

TOP RIGHT **Shutters are an unconventional alternative to standard window dressing. Graceful fretwork lets in more light and looks far more delightful than ordinary slatted panels.**

mirrors

here's looking at you

A good-sized bathroom mirror is essential to ensure that you go out into the world looking your best. Correct positioning is essential. The ideal spot is in front of a window so that there is natural light all around it. This isn't always practical, so you need to find the next best place with as much natural light as possible. Evaluate the mirror's position and look at all the elements of shape, size, and style of frame that will complement your overall look. A large mirror is an excellent way to disguise a cramped or gloomy bathroom and give the ambience and impression of more light and space than you actually have.

ABOVE **Mirror glass can be anything but plain. There's no fancy frame here to distract from the clean lines and stencil-etched Latin words of this object of desire.**

RIGHT **A generous bathroom deserves a grand mirror. This prima donna makes a stunning feature with its varnished frame and black detailing. It almost doubles the amount of light in the room.**

tip

Compensate for your lack of light with a little ingenuity. A circle cut professionally by a glazier makes the perfect opening for a small spotlight. A loose frame of iridescent glass mosaic tiles, fixed using a glue gun, surrounds this humble mirror with extra pizzazz.

how to make a towel frame

Swathed in a fresh blue and white bath towel, a humdrum frame becomes an encasement for a must-have mirror.

1. **Place the bath towel over the front of the frame, fold it around the four sides, and staple it to the back of the frame. Cut a diagonal cross in the towel where the mirror goes. Fold back the four triangles of fabric and staple these to the back of the mirror.**

2. **Cut the ribbon trim to size. Use a glue gun to fix the ribbon to the towel fabric. Fit the mirror into the frame and secure.**

storage

LEFT **A larger bathroom is a great and unexpected place to incorporate some big, handsome pieces. A freestanding ladder creates easy-to-use, accessible storage for towels and toiletries.**

RIGHT **Damp towels left on the bathroom floor drive many a mom to distraction. Give everyone their own peg, at a height they can reach, and there are no more excuses.**

RIGHT **Make the most of a single storage space by combining open chunky shelves for good-looking containers of perfumes and creams with a neat mirrored cupboard that keeps less attractive medicines and toiletries safe and out of sight.**

FAR LEFT **On top of being practical, everyday items stored creatively can make a graphic and stylish feature. Even toilet paper rolls look chic stacked up in a big glass vase.**

LEFT **Finishing touches like chic luggage labels look great and help you lay your hands on anything quickly.**

neat and tidy

Good storage is vital for a bathroom to function efficiently. There are so many items that you need to have on hand, from soaps and shampoos to talcs and toiletries. You might have spare towels, toilet paper rolls, medicines, first aid equipment, and cleaning materials all vying for space in the one room. Without a proper basket, laundry too can clutter up the bathroom. Unless you get it all organized you'll be forever searching through piles of towels and toothbrushes for the sunblock or the shower gel. When you're tired at the end of a long day or staggering sleepily from your bed in the morning, it's no fun hunting high and low for a new tube of toothpaste. Some items, like attractive soaps and bottles, are worth displaying out in the open, but others, like your bath cleaner, are probably best kept out of sight, so you need a range of different elementary storage options to keep your bathroom clear.

ABOVE RIGHT **Separating your laundry makes good sense. Having designated laundry baskets makes the job easier. Here, an existing laundry holder is stenciled and a discreet striped fabric top is added.**

RIGHT **A cart makes for really practical, mobile storage. With a few modifications, a small coffee table can be converted with casters, a coat of paint, and a series of drawer handles to hang spare towels or accessories.**

detail

ABOVE You won't even notice a standard cord and light pull, but with a little thought it's easy to have something distinctive and memorable using small pebbles and thin, rough rope.

ABOVE It takes the generous and elegant drapes, big luxurious tassels, gleaming antique chrome fittings, and the subtle relief design on the bath to achieve the sumptuous feel of this bathroom.

LEFT A fantastic floor can make a real statement. Floor paint and stencils will transform plain pine boards into a convincing impression of complicated artifact tiling.

little luxuries

Details are crucial to the success of any room. In fact, they can make or break any space, and the bathroom is no exception. Once you've established your color scheme, a careful look at the details will enhance the area and make the entire room work as a whole. It's like wearing a beautiful outfit—it's only complete with the addition of jewelry and the perfect handbag. In a bathroom, success may hinge on which light switch, toilet paper holder, flooring, or faucets you choose; each choice could either strengthen or dilute the final result. Let luxury prevail. Exquisite-looking toiletries are definitely part of the picture. Take time to select the little items carefully, as the sum of the parts will make all the difference to a polished room you'll be proud of.

BELOW **Each individual accessory is a showpiece in itself, but combined they create a look that is eye-catching and unique.**

tip

You can't beat candlelight for a seriously relaxing soak. For a real pampering, a few feminine touches really set the mood, and here it only takes the addition of two necklaces and bangles to glamorize a simple sconce.

ABOVE LEFT **Hand-painted stones act as little display gems where space is at a premium.**

ABOVE **Now every woman can freely admit to being a collecto-maniac while staying in hotels. These minitoiletries make a tangible collection displayed in the glass tank.**

LEFT **You don't need pricey or special items to make a formidable shelf display work. The key to success is in the individual visual enticement of the pieces you choose and the way that you group these items together.**

show off

Bathroom displays serve a very definite purpose. Items and objects are presented in an understated way to provide an extra, indefinable something to the look of the room, adding to the intimate impression you get when you enter. Display is the watchword! Pretty bottles and scrumptious soaps can easily be stored tidily away in cupboards, but how bland, unwelcoming, and cheerless would your bathroom be if everything was hidden?

ABOVE **Even a budget supermarket soap dispenser can be made dazzling enough to show off. Soak off the manufacturer's label, dry off the bottle, and apply stick-on skin jewelry sequins to decorate.**

LEFT **Beautiful perfume bottles and a vase of flowers set out on a small occasional table makes for a distinctly glamorous setting.**

RIGHT **Spend a quiet moment wrapping spare soaps with leftover wallpapers in muted colors and pretty satin ribbons. Finish off with large crystal chandelier drops from a flea market find. Grouped together, the chameleon soap bars are barely recognizable.**

dining spaces

topping it off

A table with a design integrated into its top definitely elevates it above the ordinary and gives you a no-wash, no-iron alternative to a tablecloth. Glass is a brilliant tabletop element, creating a functional surface with an exhibition space underneath. The large expanse is an opportunity for all kinds of display, from pebbles and coins to fabrics, lace, leaves, and photos, and you can still add a centerpiece for any occasion. Buy your glass from an experienced glazing company, letting them know exactly how you intend to use it so they can advise you on the right depth and strength of glass. You'll need to take precise measurements of the tabletop using a metal rule—fractions of an inch can make the difference between success and disaster. When in doubt, ask the professionals to measure the table for you. Also make sure to ask that the edges be polished smooth.

LEFT **The entire table has been scattered with about twenty dollars of loose change, then covered by a panel of glass. Make sure your coins are of the same width (though if a few are a bit thinner that will work as well), or rest the glass on small supports at intervals around the edge—otherwise the glass will be unsteady and could crack. Keep your budget under control by using low-value coins, or even toy money. This is also a neat way to display leftover foreign currency and remember special trips.**

LEFT **An irregular shape can make a highly unusual dining table that works just as well as a typical rectangle or oval in terms of seating a good number of people. This uniquely playful piece consists of two layers of glass with a supporting rim and a scattering of polished pebbles sandwiched between. You can clearly see the table legs and the floor below—a far cry from the traditional.**

RIGHT AND BELOW RIGHT **An old paneled door can have a surprising new life as a witty and unconventional dining table. The recessed panels form shallow trays, perfect for placing interesting items. Here, heavy old iron keys that have probably turned many locks in the past now rest below a sheet of glass. Small wooden supports at each corner of the door, the same depth as the beading, hold the glass so it is evenly balanced. Photocopies of a key create a striking monochromatic border around the walls.**

LEFT **Adapt a coffee table for Japanese-style dining with a change of seating. Instead of chairs, use floor cushions to change the scale, bringing the tabletop to the right level for eating. Oriental-type bowls and chopsticks complete the aesthetic, and are decorative even when not in use.**

dressed for company

A tablecloth can transform the drabbest piece of furniture into a dream gathering place for great meals. There are so many possibilities along with the obvious ready-made choices, and you won't need to spend a fortune to cause a stir. Some creations may last for only one event, but it's far more exciting to have a fresh, new look on occasion than to bring out the same covers every time. A range of materials and finishing touches will create the special, memorable atmosphere you want for a birthday, christening, or dinner party.

LEFT AND ABOVE **An engagement, wedding, or baby shower merits this truly exquisite voile cloth, thrown over a white-painted table, showing off the delicate, filmy fabric while a deep fringe of glittering blue glass beading weights the cloth. If your table is made of dark wood, first place a white cloth over it, or alternatively, turn the rich color to your advantage and use voiles in vibrant gold or russet that will look sensational against a darker background.**

LEFT A runner always makes a strong statement, highlighting the center area with color or pattern and revealing the tabletop or an underlying tablecloth on the sides. Set the scene for a glamorous nighttime party with a dazzling runner made from fabrics with the look of evening wear. Here, a broad strip of creamy satin forms the main body, but a deep band of gleaming gold lamé stitched to either end overhangs the sides of the table. Lamé is very easy to handle—it can be cut with scissors and won't fray, so there's no hemming involved.

BELOW LEFT AND BELOW A paper runner is inexpensive and disposable and holds myriad decorative possibilities. Investigate wallpapers with a hint of pattern—a whole roll could easily cost less than a tablecloth and is the perfect width. A crackle-glaze print, picked up for a few dollars in a sale, has been stenciled in silver with a delicate fern leaf. A generous overhang at either end shows off a striking design. If clean, the runner can be rolled up and reused; if not, it costs next to nothing to throw it away and make a fresh one, with a new stencil design, next time around.

smack in the middle

Like everything else on your table, the centerpiece should be in keeping with the style of meal you're serving and the atmosphere of the gathering. An elegant dinner with several courses will call for a very different decoration from a casual family-style supper with friends. Whatever the occasion, your centerpiece should be fresh and eye-catching, making the table attractive and interesting and setting the tone for you and your guests to relax and enjoy the meal. A stunning centerpiece doesn't have to be complicated or time-consuming—fresh flowers have a charm of their own, and with a few imaginative add-ons, you're there.

RIGHT **Fruit and flowers are the perfect, natural combination for a bright, fresh party look that you can put together in a moment. Pierce the top of an orange with a skewer and push in the stalk of a cut flower head. Half a dozen grouped on a platter will give your festive table a bold injection of energy.**

how to make sushi flowers

These exquisite iris blooms enhance the experience, whether you're serving a lavish Oriental banquet of your own making or take-out right from the boxes.

1. For each sushi iris, take a long green leaf, coil it into a miniature cylinder, and secure it with double-sided tape. Cut a small slice off one end to create a flat bottom, so the cylinder will sit on a plate. Press a piece of dampened florist's oasis inside the cylinder—this provides weight and keeps the flowers fresh.

2. Cut the iris stems carefully so that only the petals will show over the top of the leaf, then insert two or three into each piece of oasis. Tie a length of fine ribbon around each leaf, finish with a tiny knot, and place the irises on plain, flat serving dishes. Bind pairs of chopsticks with the same ribbon to complete the presentation.

ABOVE LEFT **A beautiful table center can add glamour to everyday meals. Here, a single votive candle is placed in a hurricane lantern, wedged securely in a handful of inconspicuous white pebbles. Fill the lantern with water to about halfway up the candle. Add a flash of color by taking two or three flower heads, perhaps from a plant or bouquet that's just past its prime, and tearing the petals apart to float on the water.**

RIGHT **Make the most of irresistible spring flowers with a pretty Easter look, perfect for a breakfast, lunch, or tea table. Clean out eggshells and stand them in glass eggcups. Fill each with a little water to make tiny vases for delicate seasonal blooms. Cut the stems down so that the heads just peek over the tops of the shells.**

place settings

setting the stage

Whatever mood you want to produce for your table, place settings are key. This doesn't mean spending ages arranging masses of specialized silverware, folding napkins in dramatic shapes, and making calligraphy name tags—appropriate for the rare, lavish formal dinner party—but employing just a few quick, easy, and effective ideas that tell your guests you've still put thought into the occasion.

BELOW **For an extravagant and memorable event, create a spirited theme that is carried through in every element of the table. Here, the custom-made table has been stenciled with a pattern of piano keys, and the place mats are real sheet music, singed at the edges for a hint of mystery and history. Opulent touches, such as the gold tones of the cutlery, candelabra, glassware, and china and the luscious, casually strewn bunches of grapes, all add up to this seductive musically inspired fantasy.**

BELOW RIGHT **Greenery is the ideal material to dress up a plain table in a matter of seconds. A flat, glossy leaf that virtually covers the plate lends a fresh look to stacked dishes ready for serving. A slender, striped leaf can be twined in a scroll around the most modest white napkin and held discreetly with double-sided tape. Instead of place cards, give guests their own bowls personalized with ceramic paint, which could be given away as a party favor at the end of the evening.**

BELOW FAR RIGHT **For a fresh take on standard name tags, send a message in a bottle. The names can be handwritten, or you can use a dramatic computer font. Soak the labels off of clean miniature alcohol bottles of varying sizes and use tweezers to insert the rolled-up labels, face out, before screwing the tops back on.**

how to make fruit prints

Fruit prints add a cheerful note to table fabrics like napkins or tablecloths and come out well every time, whether you're an accomplished crafter or a beginner.

1. Choose fabric paints in three complementary, natural tones, such as green, yellow, and orange. Take a hard or unripe pear with a strong, curving shape, cut it in half, and paint the inside surface in the three shades, using a fine artist's brush.

2. Place the pear, wet side down, firmly and carefully onto a corner of your napkin. Lift off to reveal a soft, three-toned image. Allow it to dry. The print will show up best on a white or cream napkin.

plate decoration

what a dish

Decorating plates adds to the distinctive look and atmosphere of a special event. You can also give that extra touch to your everyday dishes to make them more enjoyable to use. Either way, it's a surefire method of personalizing your table. Dishware ranges from the relatively inexpensive to the exorbitant, but with a few clever techniques you can elevate a budget purchase into a set you'll be proud to put out for guests.

ABOVE **For a real one-of-a-kind set, put your face or your friends' faces onto plates. Using a Polaroid photograph and a transfer kit suitable for china (from a craft shop) you can fix any image permanently onto a plate. You can also scan the picture on a computer and print it onto clear adhesive labels for onetime personalized party plates. Use pictures of the birthday girl or boy, engaged couple, or new homeowner—or better still, raid the albums for cheesy old photos of the guests of honor as kids!**

RIGHT **Ceramic paints will liven up the plainest china and also turn it into an original gift. Check the instructions on the product, since some paints have to be fired in the oven and others don't. You'll need a little artistic flair to complete some hand-panted designs, so practice before you start and choose a pattern you're confident with.**

RIGHT **A wooden salad bowl will require frequent washing that could damage any embellishment, but the matching platter on which it rests might only need a quick rinse, so take advantage and enhance it. A garnish of emerald-green glass nuggets, used by florists and adhered with a glue gun, stands out like jewels on the wood and complements a fresh, leafy salad.**

how to splatter-paint a plate

tip

If your paint requires firing, check first to see that your dishes are sufficiently ovenproof by testing one piece using the time and temperature advised on the paint label. A paint that requires firing may be easier to handle if you are a beginner—a mistake can be cleaned off with a cloth or cotton swab because the pigment isn't fixed until the china is fired.

With ceramic paint and a few palm leaves, you can transform your routine plates into out-of-the-ordinary ones.

1. **Using one leaf for each plate, coat leaves with spray adhesive and lay them carefully onto the plates, firmly pressing down along each frond.**

2. **Put dishware-friendly paint into a shallow bowl. Use an old paintbrush with splayed-out bristles (gently spread the bristles of a new one). Dip it in the paint, hold it at an angle over newspaper, and tap the handle sharply against the handle of a wooden spoon to knock the excess off. Use the same method to spatter fine paint droplets over the plate. When the plate is dry, peel off the leaf and fire if necessary.**

glassware

sheer brilliance

To transform glass from the mundane to the magnificent you need to add color. The combination of light and vibrant hues gives painted or embellished glass its jewel-like appeal. Glass paints are quick and easy to use at home and will invigorate any plain piece. Painting glasses for drinks adds a glorious touch to a celebration, but they can be fragile and will really only stand up to infrequent use. Glass items such as bowls, plates, and flasks also lend themselves to decoration for particular occasions.

how to paint a decanter

This opaque decanter has an attractive shape, but a painted grass effect gives it an extra helping of charisma.

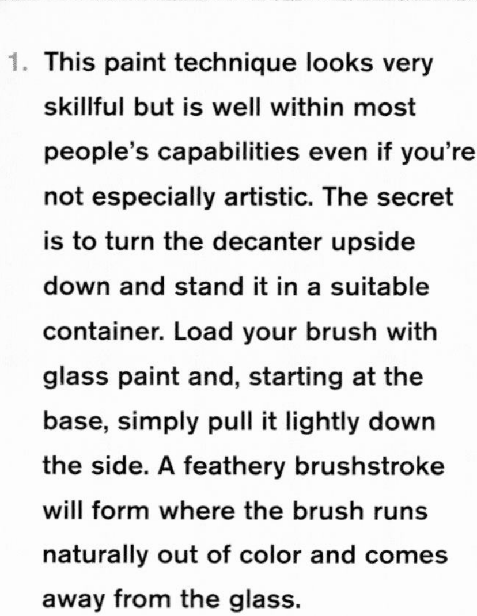

1. This paint technique looks very skillful but is well within most people's capabilities even if you're not especially artistic. The secret is to turn the decanter upside down and stand it in a suitable container. Load your brush with glass paint and, starting at the base, simply pull it lightly down the side. A feathery brushstroke will form where the brush runs naturally out of color and comes away from the glass.

2. Work all around the decanter. You can either apply the darker green first, then go around again highlighting with yellow or lime, or apply the two tones together using separate brushes. Any mistakes as you start will end up inconspicuously near the base.

RIGHT **This unusual decoration adds substance and depth to an incredibly delicate, slender glass candleholder, using jewelry wire and a combination of three beads of different sizes and colors. A length of wire is wrapped around a pencil to make a fine spiral that can be threaded with a random assortment of beads. The wire is loosely coiled around the candlestick, with a smaller piece wound around the top. The result is a modern filigree effect with a 3-D quality.**

LEFT **Why not keep a special bowl for your favorite fruit? A clear glass bowl and plate won't set you back more than a few dollars. Use a cotton swab to dot them with glass paints for a fresh, summery look that picks up the colors of perfectly rippened fruit. Though applying the paint is easy, try it out on paper first to get the hang of it. Use a separate palette on each item, perhaps reds and oranges for the bowl and blues and purples for the plate. The finish is permanent and doesn't need firing.**

presentation

mouthwatering

So much of our appreciation of food is visual. Imaginatively presented, a dessert, sandwich, or perhaps just a sliced apple will seem so much more enjoyable than the same food served on a practical but boring white paper plate. Clever presentation needn't take much time, yet it can whet your appetite and transform dinner, whether a homemade feast or take-out, into a banquet.

how to make an ice bowl

An ice bowl encasing delicate flower heads and leaves takes little time to prepare and is a heavenly way to serve ordinary sorbet, fruit salad, or ice cream.

1. **You need two freezer-safe bowls. They must be the same shape, but the smaller one should fit inside the larger one with a gap of about ½ to 1 inch all around. Place the larger one in the sink, add water, and place the smaller one inside. Pour sugar (because it's heavy and you can pour it in gradually) into the small bowl, weighing it down until it is floating about 1 inch above the base of the large bowl. Some of the water will flow over the rim when the sugar is poured in.**

2. **Place flowers and leaves into the water between the bowls. Single blooms will just float, but you can make long, slender, flexible leaves like chives encircle the frozen bowl if you add them first. Then arrange the flower heads and sprigs of greenery. Put the bowls in the freezer. Several hours before your guests arrive, remove them from the freezer and leave them to sit for about ten minutes. Gently lift out the inner bowl, then turn upside down and slide off the outer one. Put the ice bowl back in the freezer in an upright position. When you're ready, just add the dessert and set it on a plate with a few extra flowers just before serving.**

LEFT **Make a frozen meringue look like you've spent hours rather than minutes in the kitchen. Place the meringue on a generously sized circular platter, top it with fresh raspberries, surround it with blueberries, and sift confectioner's sugar over the fruit. Present it ringed by mini terra-cotta pots, each with a lighted candle.**

tip

For safety, contain the whole display on a tray. Blow out and remove the candles before actually serving the dessert, and keep the flames well away from children, pets, and flammable fabrics like curtains, tablecloths, or napkins.

LEFT **A light serving of fruit could look meager, but not if you don't skimp on the presentation. A small, deep bowl showcases a handful of plums in an appetizing mound. Placed on an oversized square charger, space remains for exotic leaves and a single, perfect bloom in a tiny holder. With one green leaf from the garden laid atop the plums—so fresh—who could resist?**

home offices

tip

A living room corner can easily go to waste, but a desk can readily fit in without compromising the main relaxation area. A screen gives a sense of separation without leaving you feeling uncomfortably enclosed, especially if you can glimpse the room beyond, either over the top or through a gap.

LEFT **A living room can be divided unobtrusively into work and leisure zones. This entire space uses a single palette of gentle greens mixed with wood, but a change of stain on the floorboards provides a subtle demarcation between the two functions. A decorative wooden screen marks the boundary of the work area. Freestanding office storage units are on view but, camouflaged in soft shades that blend with the decor, they don't stand out from the overall feel of the room.**

LEFT **Decide what tools you need on hand and create appealing, easy-to-use storage receptacles to accommodate them. An unused corner of the desk can be enlivened with small pots for pencils, scissors, pens, or whatever you require.**

a room for all reasons

Saying good-bye to miserable commuting and bad-tempered bosses is immensely appealing, but naturally there's a trade-off. At the end of a busy day at the office, you leave work and head for home, but when home and office become one, you'll find that both gearing up and shutting down take a bit more planning. A home work area has to function efficiently in terms of comfort and convenience and motivate you to get down to business. This isn't too difficult when you have a separate room for an office—the trouble starts when one space has to fulfill two or even three purposes—you can't relax or entertain in a living room full of files and folders; nor can you concentrate on your work if you're surrounded by clothes, breakfast dishes, or books and magazines.

Working from home raises singular decorating issues. But it also gives you a unique opportunity to tailor your environment to personally suit the way you work, so include the things you like to have around you, dispense with the things you don't, and make it as enjoyable as a workplace can get.

LEFT AND ABOVE **Don't get boxed in! You might feel shut away behind a solid screen, so give yourself a window onto the room beyond. Circular cutout openings inset with a wooden leaf shape give a vista outside your work area and allow you to feel included without distracting you from your work.**

Try to appropriate one of the windows, too. You'll benefit from good natural light, perhaps a view, and certainly a more pleasant atmosphere.

LEFT **A dining table covered with a large-scale map topped with glass can double as a complete home office for frequent-flyers. There's room on the table for a laptop, phone, and all the tools needed for planning and booking trips. After hours, the area serves as the route to the stairs as well as the dining room, and the map remains an intriguing tabletop feature.**

desks and storage

laying the foundation

A desk is one of the key pieces of furniture in a home office. Check factors like height and width and think about the objects you want in and on your desk. For example, a laptop and mobile phone won't swallow up nearly as much space as a fixed computer terminal and an integrated phone and fax machine. Think about whether you need drawers, how large they should be to accommodate your supplies, and on which side they should be. The positioning of your desk is also worth a few minutes' thought. Place it in front of a window and you'll either thrive on the daylight pouring in or spend too much time gazing out, wondering what everyone else is doing. Would you prefer empty space in front of you, or a wall for a bulletin board and shelves with files immediately at hand? Do you have enough conveniently positioned power outlets and phone jacks for your office machines, without having electric cords trailing around the floor, and without overloading your power source? You might find the ideal desk in an office furniture store, but perhaps the right desk for you isn't a desk at all—you may realize that an ordinary table or maybe even a make-up table fits the bill. Or you may have specific criteria that can only be met by having a unit custom-built.

It's important to decide how to store papers, too. Filing cabinets will do the job but aren't great to look at when an office is sharing space in a living room or bedroom. Infrequently needed items can perhaps be archived, but for ongoing paperwork you'll want to create storage solutions that blend into the decor of your home.

LEFT AND BELOW **A subdued palette helps you concentrate, undistracted by loud patterns or eye-catching colors. A broad brush loaded with contrasting glaze and dragged first vertically and then horizontally across a desk creates a subtle rattan effect and shows how to add interest with restful hues. The ledge and wall in front of the desk, displaying work-related objects and unusual personal items, all in mellow tones, keep this space ordered and tranquil.**

tip

Hide files you don't need daily access to under wraps in your living room, hallway, or bedroom. A cover of fake-suede fabric with a fixed lace-up detail can slide over a conventional metal filing cabinet and transform it into a smart side table, topped with glass and a few well-chosen ornamental pieces. To access the contents occasionally, remove the glass and slip off the cover.

make it homey

When you work in an office building you have to put up with someone else's choice of decor, furniture, and even paper clips and staplers. And it's inevitably the dreariest, most functional, and unstylish stuff on the market. Your home office can have a much more relaxed atmosphere than a corporate space. As long as the job gets done, you can have music, radio, or even television if you wish, work the hours that suit you, and wear pajamas and eat ice cream at your desk when you like. Small touches, like a funky filing tray or brightly hued stapler will remind you just how good it feels to be in charge. The color of your ink, the style of your stationery, and even the message on your answering machine reflect your personality and the image of your business.

It's helpful to have separate phone lines for work and personal calls. You'll always know, depending on which phone rings, whether to expect a friend or a work contact on the line.

LEFT **Attractive office furniture can only improve your performance. A cozy blanket chair cover means you still have the support you need from a good chair, but a prettier place to sit. If you share your home with pets, let them join you at work, too. Stroke a cat after a difficult phone call—it's a great de-stressing technique! Dogs, too, prefer being around their owners all day to staying home alone and will force you to take breaks during the working day for walks and so on. You'll both feel much better for it.**

tip

Items that aren't specifically designed for business use can often be very helpful on the job, while looking much more appealing than customary office tools. A chic greeting card holder makes an ideal place for keeping important phone numbers or addresses safe, and you can intersperse work-related notes and papers with a photo or personal card.

BELOW **If you like buying flowers for the living room or bedroom, why not treat your office to a bunch, too? Since you will probably spend much of your day there, you'll have plenty of opportunity to enjoy them, and fresh flowers are unbeatable for softening the surroundings.**

BELOW **Fill empty shelf space with something you'll enjoy looking at. Cacti make great work-mates since they need next to no maintenance to stay green and fresh. Add a dash of humor—plant them in cups and saucers instead of the usual pots.**

bulletin boards

ABOVE **Propped against the wall, a colored acrylic sheet makes an inexpensive board that lets you see the color behind while you write on the front. It's as easy to clean as an ordinary dry erase board, but will make your office appear much more modern and less functional.**

at a glance

A bulletin board is an essential element in any workspace and there are plenty to choose from, so you can find one perfectly matched to your specific needs. To function effectively your bulletin board must be the right size for the information you want to keep on it, and must also have a layout that suits you. You might want flexible space for lists or reminders that change daily or even hourly. Perhaps you require room for notes that move around as work progresses, or a safe place to pin receipts or other valuable paperwork. Standard bulletin boards are usually square or rectangular and pretty uninspiring. If you create your own, it can take any shape you like, and needn't have any straight lines at all. It can be made from a whole range of materials, as long as you can write on it smoothly or attach what you need quickly. The items on a hardworking bulletin board are constantly changing, so make sure it's easy to clear it properly too, so that it doesn't become a magnet for clutter.

LEFT **With blackboard paint your memo board can fit anywhere you choose and be absolutely any shape or size you fancy. Lying completely flush to the wall, it almost forms part of the decoration, so forget sensible squares and grab the chance to make your personal mark. For an intricate design, cut a card or paper template first and use masking tape for a really neat finish.**

RIGHT **Clothespins are almost made for the job of keeping important phone numbers and reminders from going astray. Unlike standard office clips, they don't have a heavy spring that can be awkward to open. Their size and shape make them especially easy to handle in a system that involves moving slips of paper from one pin to another.**

tip

An acrylic picture frame can be turned into a fun to-do board for the office. Use letter transfers to write the days of the week in any order you like, then add sticky notes of all your jobs. At the end of the week, just pull them all off, ready for next Monday morning.

containers

everything in its place

Containers keep your office running efficiently, whether they group your important files together or stop your paper clips from tumbling all over your desk. You can design containers for your home office that suit your particular working methods and help make your day run as smoothly as possible. Don't waste time labeling containers. Instead, make the containers themselves clear visual signals that tell you instantly what's inside. One particular project or client's papers could go in yellow folders, and another in blue, so you can quickly locate the right information. If, for example, you use a white-painted terra-cotta pot for pencils and a green one for pens, the containers encourage you to put things away and keep surfaces clear.

Containers also let you indulge your personality. For a hint of glamour try gold and silver spray paints on different drawers of a filing cabinet, or line filing trays with shimmering wrapping paper in strong jewel shades, again choosing different colors to let you know what's in each one.

FAR LEFT **Turn a tame-looking container into something glamorous. With a glue gun and a handful of glistening glass nuggets, your undistinguished pencil holder becomes a bejewelled beauty.**

LEFT **Bold visual clues, be they a spread of shades or individual trims like ribbons, tassels, symbols, or pictures, are far easier to read than labels. To make a stack of identical filing drawers more user-friendly, pick a fresh palette that's easy on the eye and paint each drawer separately. Putting your hand on the one you want right away will soon become second nature**

RIGHT **Shiny silver minibrioche baking tins are the perfect containers for small items like paper clips, erasers, and pushpins in order. Line the drawer first with bright wrapping paper to make the tins stand out.**

tip

Left as the manufacturer intended, you'd have to check inside each of these plain wooden box files to find the one you want. Three different tones indicate separate purposes, and the code could be carried through to other related items in the office. Dipped in fabric dye and left to dry, the boxes become subtly shaded from pale at the top to deep at the base; grouped together they make an attractive display.

notebooks

LEFT A pair of wood-veneered sheets, punched and threaded with rough string, make a tough and distinctive book cover. Choose lighter or darker woods to identify the contents.

BELOW LEFT Something as simple as a postcard or photo glued on the front will set your folders apart. The pictures needn't even relate to what's inside—just choose images you like to have around. When they're up on a shelf, colored ribbons will help identify them.

BELOW For a 3-D effect that's lovely to touch, cut bold letters or shapes from an old blanket or sweater and attach them to the cover of a plain, store-bought notebook using iron-on adhesive backing.

note to self

You'll probably have several notebooks at work that you value highly and refer to on a regular basis. Perhaps there's one for phone numbers, another for meeting notes, a third for drawings and plans, and maybe a fourth for calculations and financial information. Imagine they all look identical in size, color, and shape and then think how much time and energy you'd waste trying to find the right one every time you needed to check or enter something. Typed labels on the fronts might help, but besides being incredibly unexciting they're difficult to see at a glance. Visual stimuli inspire the quickest response, so distinctive covers, pictures on the front, and trims like bright ribbon and rich braid will ensure that you go straight to the one you want instead of sifting through the stack to find it. You needn't label the front with the name of what's inside—a postcard of a favorite view, a photo of your pet or partner, or a lively pink and gold ribbon can just as easily distinguish one notebook from another and will give you so much more pleasure than a drab, utilitarian sticker.

how to decorate a notebook

It takes hardly any craft skill to transform a basic fabric-covered notebook into a luxurious office accessory. Pick a striking color and personalize the front with a selection of vivid satin ribbons and fancy braiding attached with fabric glue.

FedEx Express BOX
Pull to open
Medium
FedEx Federal Express BOX
FedEx Express

foyers

entryways

first impressions

As the first step into your home, the foyer, or entryway, is an important space with a unique role to play. Even though you won't stay there long, you'll pick up an immediate impression of the whole house. If it's warm, welcoming, and distinctive, both you and your guests will feel relaxed and at ease as soon as you enter, while a cold, stark, or disorganized space comes across as inhospitable and dispiriting. Color, flooring, lighting, and furniture all set the scene. The foyer is like the core of the home, the pivotal point from which the other rooms branch off, providing glimpses of the rest of the house. And from those rooms you'll still be aware of the hallway, so its look should be connected with what lies beyond in ambience, color, and style. Foyers have to function efficiently, too, coping with coats, bags, strollers, and shoes. You need pegs, racks, and closets to keep everything in order. Other useful elements are a mirror to check your appearance as you dash out and designated spots for keys and mail.

ABOVE LEFT **Don't settle for a boring boxlike foyer when a curved false wall can add impact and character to the tiniest space. A spotlight illuminates a sculpture in the recessed alcove, bathing it in a gentle glow, and with the muted terra-cotta of the walls gives a sense of warmth. African slate, wonderfully practical flooring that looks sensational, glints with natural flecks of gray, gold, and green. The swath of tiles accentuates the sweep into the apartment.**

LEFT **Even in a brand-new home, the foyer can radiate a timeless, tranquil lived-in feel. Warm, natural, and tactile, wood paneling can add depth and substance to plain walls. A neat wood console table and peg rack in various wood tones give a contemporary twist to the rustic look.**

ABOVE Color and texture on the walls give a foyer something to say without being overpowering. A sheeny ocher color wash and glimmering copper-leaf highlights instantly make the space feel cozy and inviting, yet stylish. The prominent positioning of an architecturally cut vase with a rough, sandy surface gives a strong focal point and plays on contrasting textures. And no hallway is really complete without a mirror. Everyone will appreciate the chance for a quick once-over as they pass through. A large mirror is also an exceptional way to introduce extra light and will help a dark or narrow area feel twice as spacious.

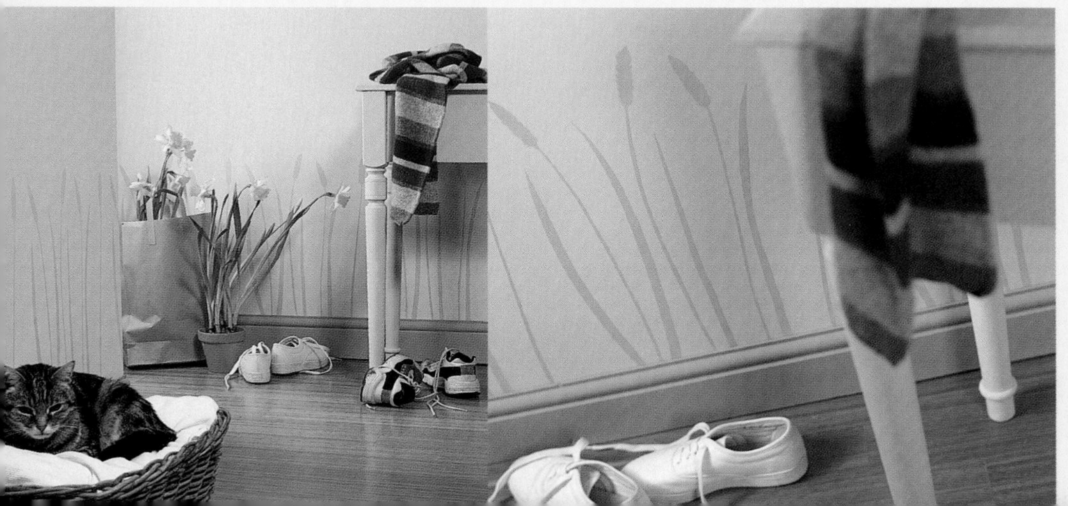

LEFT Don't ignore all that space around your knees! In an area with little furniture, the lowest third of a hallway wall is exposed and clamoring for some decoration. Go for a sizable design—try a fresh, naturally shaped stencil that won't dominate but will lead you gently through to the rest of your home.

a step above

A staircase is one of the biggest and most significant structures in a building. Every day, as you travel from one level to another or from the social to the private zones of your home, you use the stairs over and over, yet you rarely give them a second thought. Staircases have the potential to be an out-of-the-ordinary center of attention. Aside from the steps themselves, balustrades, spindles, newels, and walls can all be decorated and detailed: capitalize on them with ingenious lighting, surprising patterns, and a mass of different materials. Where money is no object, an awesome glass, metal, or wood construction can take your breath away, but spectacular stairs needn't cost a fortune. Budget tools like stencils and pens and paper can transform the most modest staircase into a real extrovert.

ABOVE **Imagine having a glass staircase. It could be yours, but you'll need to call in the professionals and the bank manager. With an expert glass structural engineer and a top-flight glazier you can produce an electrifying centerpiece in your home. Embellished with stylish etched words and tiny fiber-optic beams in each tread, this is truly a stairway to heaven. If you don't want to blow your entire home-decorating budget on the staircase, however, you can capture the essence of the idea by stenciling some wording onto wooden stairs.**

LEFT, ABOVE, AND BELOW RIGHT **Working on stairs requires patience and planning, whether you're painting the stairs themselves or the walls alongside. One flight could take up to three days, during which time people will still need to go up and down. To minimize the disruption, find a time when the house will be as empty as possible. Use quick-drying paint that will be dry to the touch in about thirty minutes and hard after two to three hours. Work from the top down, unless you want to be marooned upstairs. Even if you're not particularly artistic you can still produce great results using stencils. Secure them with masking tape to ensure crisp edges. Practice first on paper to gain confidence and plan the sequence of colors before starting in on the real thing.**

ABOVE **A staircase can set the tone for what lies ahead as it guides you from one set of surroundings to the next. With a slate floor, foliage, and terra-cotta pots this foyer has a definite natural outdoor flavor that links it strongly with the garden. Plush blue-carpeted stairs leading up to the living room make the transition, signaling the start of the interior living area.**

private collection

The hallway is an open invitation to hang art. Unlike a living room or bedroom, there's little furniture or accessories around for pictures to clash with. It makes an ideal location for themed collections like theater posters or other memorabilia. Since they are contained in a smaller space, they can make a very strong impact and be regularly enjoyed. Alternatively, those empty walls could prompt you to create something uniquely personal—items like old family photos, antique fabrics, dried leaves, or other treasures you've gathered and haven't known what to do with can now become fascinating works of art.

Pictures often end up too high on the wall, where no one can really see them properly. There's a simple skill to positioning art properly—hang it just at eye level. To hang a group of pictures, work up, down, and out from this point.

tip

Before you take a hammer and nail to the wall, cut newspaper to the sizes and shapes of your art and tack the pieces up with removable adhesive. You can easily move them around till you find the best positions. Then you're ready to hang your actual pieces.

LEFT **Make inexpensive art from what you already have. Scan old photographs into a computer or photocopy them to avoid damaging the originals, and add photocopied fabric, old newspaper, gift wrap, or even a flag for an unusual background. Here, painted wood frames hold black-and-white pictures mounted on a plaid tartan backing—there's no mistaking the Scottish heritage.**

RIGHT **Large, dyed pale blue skeleton leaves from a craft shop make a striking show, spray-glued onto a series of three neutral-colored boards. The smaller natural leaves dotted on the wall behind give weight to the display and add a finishing flourish.**

BELOW LEFT **Simplicity can be the key to making a statement. White-painted frames melt into the wall, focusing your eye on the dried fern leaves mounted on cream matboard. The frames are carefully positioned with wide gaps to echo the steps and the Shaker-influenced walls.**

BELOW CENTER **Jazz up a budget picture frame by fringing it all around with inch-long twig matchsticks. You only need a postcard or photo, a glue gun, and shears to put a natural touch on the wall.**

BELOW RIGHT **The way you hang a picture can say as much as the image itself. Framed prints bought in a shop may look very ordinary, but you can give them new interest by displaying a few hung from chains suspended from a chrome pole.**

pretty organized

Details are the layer of polish that makes a space come alive. Every hallway has the opportunity for a few well-considered extras, both visual and practical. Functionally, foyers must keep the entrance to your home organized and appealing, so visitors aren't greeted by a confusion of coats, boots, and briefcases. A console table or at the very least a ledge or shelf for mail and other odds and ends is a must. This is especially important if you share an apartment with roommates—no one needs their letters or newspapers to get buried in a communal heap. Keys are always begging to be lost, but a designated spot in the hallway can keep them under control. You may not always feel secure labeling keys, but it's easy to add identifying touches without giving away which doors they open.

BELOW **A deep mail tray stops letters from going astray once they reach your home. Make sure yours is big enough to hold the magazines or catalogues that arrive along with your mail. Add another for outgoing letters.**

BELOW **A gilded, embellished picture frame makes a glamorous storage spot for keys. Fix hooks inside and differentiate the keys with colored ribbon or labels. Alternatively, allot a different area inside the frame for each zone in the house.**

RIGHT **Roommates will love having their own bags for the daily delivery of letters and newspapers. Fix a Polaroid snapshot of each person to the outside so you know which bag belongs to whom.**

BELOW **Leave an attractive bowl in the hallway for keys and you'll always know where to find them. A pretty tassel tells you, and only you, which one opens the safe! Put a little thought into choosing the color and look of these small items—they'll build into a story of their own.**

tip

It's easy to decorate your foyer with the most charismatic key holders and mail trays, but only you can make the space function efficiently. You'll need to use the items in a disciplined way to ensure that letters and keys still don't go astray.

naturally welcoming

There's nothing like greenery for adding life and freshness to any space. Rather than a single, sad-looking specimen, treat a small foyer to a selection of green plants grouped in a variety of heights, shapes, tones, and textures. A sizable area is perfect for something that will give new arrivals something to talk about the minute they come in. Think about huge, glossy green palms to flank a doorway, picture, or mirror, or a spectacular flower arrangement that fills a table and adds an aromatic note. Remember, though, that you rarely linger in the foyer, and that plants and flowers do need looking after. Ask yourself how much time and attention you're prepared to lavish on them. If the answer is "not very much," don't despair—fuss-free alternatives are available, too.

A foyer is also the perfect place to add to the thrill and atmosphere of a party or celebration by decorating with special touches. Have some fun choosing clever seasonal details to greet your guests as they step inside your home.

LEFT **Recycled glass coffee jars, sauce bottles, and wine bottles, painted black and filled with twigs, make a dramatic silhouette against warm yellow walls. Dried pussy willow and other kinds of flowering branches last forever, so it's easy to change types of twigs three or four times a year to suit the season.**

RIGHT **With a busy schedule that doesn't allow time to care for plants and flowers, one of the best options is a dried moss topiary tree, which needs no maintenance. Buy foam balls and dried moss from a florist and add a chunky branch to make your own undemanding natural sculpture.**

ABOVE LEFT **If you love fresh flowers but can't handle the hassle, treat yourself to an orchid. One elegant bloom will single-handedly radiate chic serenity for about eight weeks, so it's great value for the money, and always stunning.**

ABOVE CENTER **Increase the air of anticipation on a special occasion. Dress up a door handle by suspending a selection of small intricate glass bottles, each with a single flowering stem, on pretty ribbons. Choose garden blooms for a casual, artless look.**

ABOVE RIGHT **If you're likely to buy fresh flowers every week, why not create a designated display spot where you can really show them off? A mirror behind a shelf multiplies a bunch into a bouquet.**

gathered together

A display should make your short stay in the foyer as enjoyable and interesting as possible and give your eye somewhere pleasant to rest. A roomy entrance can make a great place for collections—more abstract displays such as a large sculpture or a huge portrait, or unusual objects like a rocking horse or an antique gramophone—that may seem out of place in a living room or bedroom. In a smaller space, repetition is a useful device: a stack of chunky shelves or a regular row of mirrors, vases, or other items along a wall or shelf adds impact. The furniture in a foyer also creates its own display. Your console table should be at home with your coatrack, mirror, mail tray, and chair to create a harmonious picture.

ABOVE LEFT **For a small collection, like a group of vases, figures, or boxes, a hallway window ledge is a winning location. Your pieces benefit from brilliant natural lighting and, framed together, just a few objects become meaningful. Taller items can also provide extra privacy.**

LEFT **Serious consideration has been given to this narrow display space to one side of a door. Each distinctive ceramic piece sits deliberately on its own solid shelf, while the shelves themselves give the illusion of being threaded onto a steel tension wire that links the ceiling to the floor.**

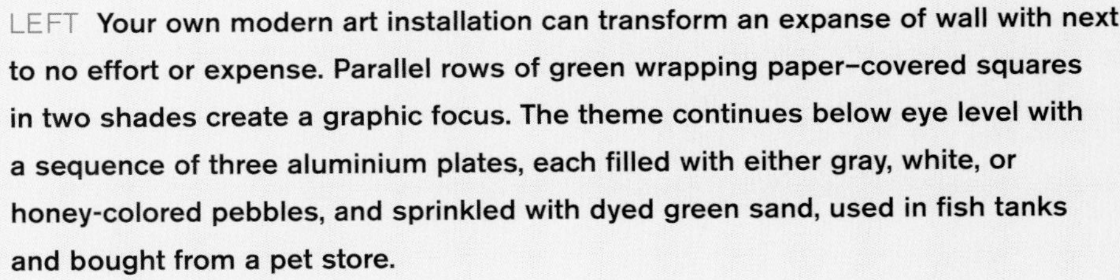

LEFT Your own modern art installation can transform an expanse of wall with next to no effort or expense. Parallel rows of green wrapping paper–covered squares in two shades create a graphic focus. The theme continues below eye level with a sequence of three aluminium plates, each filled with either gray, white, or honey-colored pebbles, and sprinkled with dyed green sand, used in fish tanks and bought from a pet store.

BELOW No one actually needs three mirrors, but as a series laid out along a burnt-orange wall, reflecting a trio of vases filled with dried leaves, they earn their place. A row of fallen branches compounds the autumnal theme and also hides a radiator while allowing warm air to circulate freely.

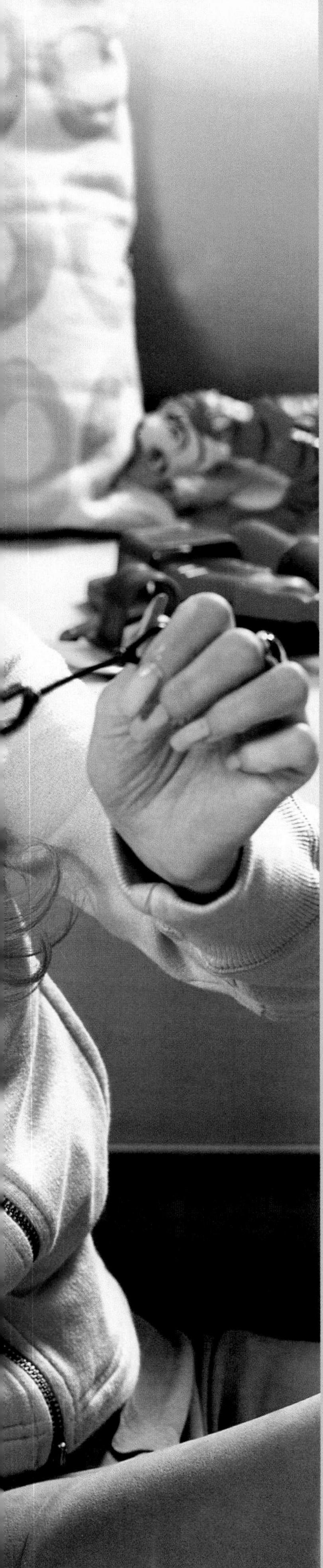

kid's zone

baby

ABOVE AND RIGHT **Make a whole play area from an ordinary bookcase. Pick bright colors and add inventive cutout doors for a doll's house or castle. Line one compartment with removable fake fur for added texture. When it's outgrown, just change the doors and repaint for a new look. One piece of furniture could see your baby through to college!**

LEFT **If your baby's room has running water, it's an ideal opportunity to get a carpenter to build a deluxe bathing and changing area with showstopping flexibility. Make sure it's the right height for your comfort and put down water-resistant flooring, like vinyl, with a dramatic and fun cutout shape. Just because this area is functional is no excuse for it to be bland. Here you see an up-to-the-minute flooring look.**

RIGHT **Small babies spend hours lying on their backs and things can get really boring for them. You try looking at a ceiling for thirty minutes! You can easily make a wondrous mobile full of movement with an ever-changing, abundant array of objects—fake flowers, bells, leaves, colorful plastic or card shapes, small squashy toys, and ribbons. (Make sure that all items are child-safe and are secured correctly.)**

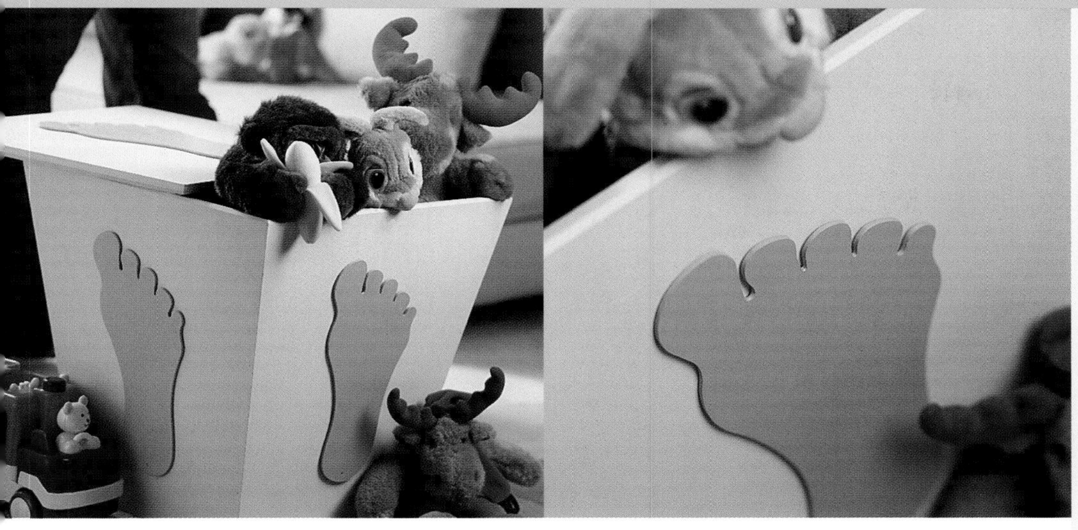

LEFT **A streamlined storage box was decorated with monster-sized cutout feet, making it an adventure for little ones to tidy up. For a simpler version, why not let them paint the soles of their own feet and print with them? Finish off by protecting the creation with a layer of fast-drying varnish. Ensure that both the paint and varnish are child-safe.**

room to grow

Babies and small children are fascinated by just about everything that's going on. Their minds are constantly piecing together a picture of the world around them, and they need plenty to look at, touch, listen to, and even chew on! Little children's rooms should be safe but stimulating, with enough shapes, sounds, movement, and color to keep them interested, even if that means sacrificing some of your own personal taste. Parents-to-be often rush out and raid the nearest baby store, spending a small fortune on so-called essentials, many of which you just don't need. Think before you make substantial purchases. A chest of drawers can double as a changing area. A homemade mobile or storage unit will be more innovative and less expensive than anything you'll find in a store. The room needs to grow along with the child and baby items can be restrictive as well as expensive, and the room could end up stuck in a baby-age time warp. Practicality is also a priority—dirty hands and crayoned walls are a fact of life, so make sure you create wipe-clean surfaces.

tip

A craze may come and go before the latest diaper hits the market. Inexpensive accessories like lamps, bedding, cushions, a clock, or a rug can easily add interest and pull together a kid's room with zest without breaking the bank.

the biggest canvas

Kids' bedroom walls are an opportunity waiting to happen. Where else can you really get away with technicolor paint schemes alongside sensational stencils, fabulous stickers, and glittery sparkles? Paint is the perfect medium. Even though it can last for years, it is one of the easiest elements of a room to change again and again. Paint is the least expensive way to implement a kaleidoscopic impact, offering you limitless color options. Sometimes, just changing one wall or adding stencils, stripes, or a border is enough to bring new life to a tired room. And painting is simple enough that you and even your kids can tackle it on your own.

ABOVE **Along with bold, colorful furniture, a really big, lively mural, which would be overpowering in any other space, is ideal for a child's room.**

BELOW LEFT **Both boys and girls will just love these fun splat designs in random colors. Choose a bright base shade and pick out accent colors from the room for the contrasting stenciled splats.**

LEFT **Even if you think you have no artistic talent whatsoever, it takes just a little time, patience, and a few small pots of paint to turn a plain wall into eye-catching art.**

BELOW LEFT **Closet doors don't need six wiggly handles when two straight ones will do, but kids love anything with a twist of the unexpected, so why not?**

tip

Preserve your children's masterpieces forever. Trim one of their best paintings and have it laminated to make a cheery backsplash for the sink.

LEFT CENTER **Add some sparkle to the walls or furniture of a little kid's room. Silver or gold glitter mixed with acrylic varnish is a fast and simple way to get things sparkling forever.**

LEFT **With a square of silver leaf and a silver felt-tip marker, it's easy to create a shimmering design that needs almost no decorating know-how.**

art

RIGHT **Tiny teddies glued around a frame create a three-dimensional border that makes a simple photograph look really special in a little girl's room.**

FAR RIGHT **Little boys just can't resist all kinds of rubbery reptiles. Put a fun card in a cheap frame, then use a glue-gun to decorate it with a whole lizard family.**

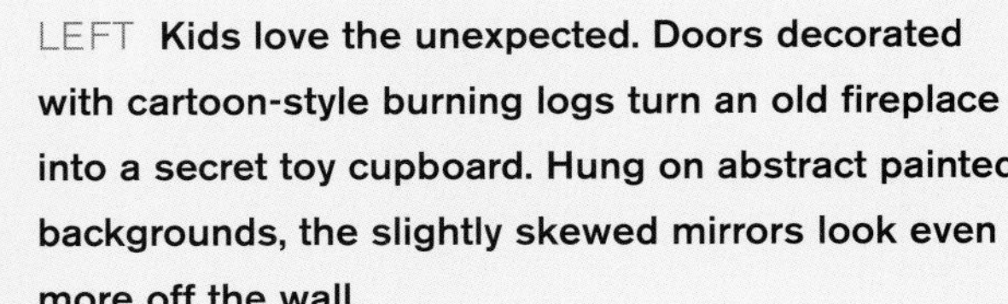

LEFT **Kids love the unexpected. Doors decorated with cartoon-style burning logs turn an old fireplace into a secret toy cupboard. Hung on abstract painted backgrounds, the slightly skewed mirrors look even more off the wall.**

BELOW LEFT **A startling and fun floor can singlehandedly metamorphose a whole room. Spots are so easy to do and look just right; you just need plates of various sizes to draw around for templates. Use a specialized floor paint and varnish for a long-lasting finish.**

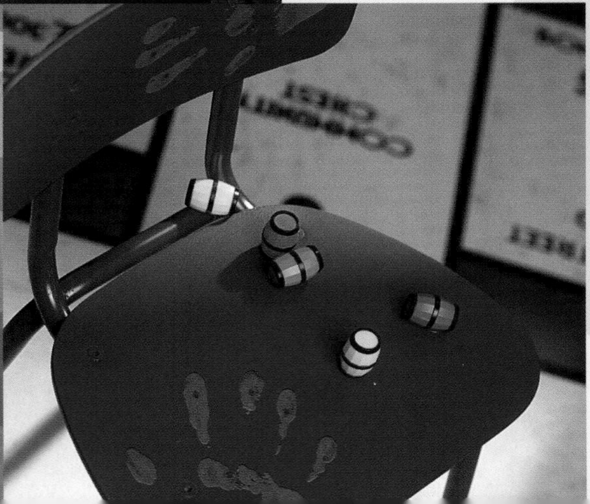

tip

Give your child a chance to make his mark. An ordinary chair becomes a child's treasured possession when given a personal printed stamp of approval. Choose two cheerful, contrasting colors for hands or feet. Finish off with a coat of acrylic varnish. (Again, make sure paint and varnish are child-safe.)

freedom of expression

Everyone has heard that plaintive moan, "I'm bored!" Children soak up stimuli like sponges and constantly need things to interest and engage them. The bedrooms and playrooms where they spend time have to feed their imaginations with the help of color, shapes, textures, and ideas that challenge and excite them. Kids' rooms should be full of child-style fun that appeals on their level, not yours. Let them stamp their personality onto color schemes, furniture, accessories, and even the floor, if they want to. The more the room feels like theirs, the more they'll enjoy playing there.

BELOW **Two kids, two chairs, which is whose? Avoid a fight—use the same colors but different patterns to make a matching pair that won't get mixed up.**

how to paint a chair

1. **Lightly sand the chair, wipe it down, and apply primer. Allow it to dry. Paint the chair with a water-based latex color. Allow it to dry.**
2. **Use masking tape to mark off your design. Paint one color at a time, remove the masking tape while the paint is still tacky, and allow it to dry. Continue until your design is complete.**
3. **Apply several coats of water-based varnish to protect the paint. Ensure that all the paints you use are child-friendly.**

a room of her own

If there's one thing teenage girls are very sure about, it's everything—including their own taste. They know just what's hot, what's not, what's cool, what's in, and what's out. Whether she is a head-to-toe know-it-all fashion babe or a wannabe rock star, the style of clothes she goes for can give some clue to her dream room. Young girls tend to love anything really feminine, so safe bets are flowers, beading, fake fur, and sparkle, but, as any mom will tell you, the best move is to let them loose, choose for themselves, and do it themselves. If they think you like it too, they may feel obliged to hate it on principle. Moms and dads just aren't cool!

tip

Most teenagers love to recycle, so save old jam jars to make this quick fix jewelry holder. Decorate the lids with fake flower heads using a glue gun.

how to make a flower pillow

You need minimal sewing skills to dress up inexpensive cushions. A clean-cut daisy design is very fresh and adds a feminine touch to a bed or sofa.

1. **Make templates for the petals and center from the card.**
2. **Cut the shapes out of felt using the templates as a guide.**
3. **Sew the pieces onto plain cushions with bright, contrasting wool using big stitches.**

ABOVE **Dull closet doors are not what a girl wants. Using existing doors, cut out randomly spaced circles with an electric jigsaw, then back the inside of each door with dyed muslin, which will show through the holes.**

BELOW **Adorn plain voiles with fake red-fabric roses and play up the romantic look. First pin the flowers on carefully to get the right positions, then attach each one with a couple of stitches. She'll love it, and it's easy to change when a new color is needed.**

ABOVE **Terra-cotta pots given a makeover make very cool storage for small items. Paint on any design, stencil on words, or stick on pictures, sequins, and beading. Finish them off with an extravagant trim around the top.**

ABOVE RIGHT **Girls need a place for all their make-up paraphernalia, but nothing too conventional will do. An old paint can, thoroughly cleaned out and decorated with sequins, makes a great cosmetics container. And when one is full, it's just as easy to make another.**

CENTER RIGHT **An old picture frame from a flea market and some strips of torn tissue paper, combined with romantic words written in gold felt-tip pen, add up to a Hollywood-style wall treatment that doesn't cost a fortune in money or time.**

RIGHT **Creating the right mood for a teenage girl's room doesn't have to mean a floor-to-ceiling rethink. Some pretty bedding and embellished cushions will add the gloss and sophistication she wants.**

teen boys

LEFT **Boys tend to go for beds with a confident design and a strong, masculine edge. Try accessories like these khaki green and denim cushions.**

RIGHT **Most boys could successfully tackle making a simple row of boxes with circular fronts, for storing CDs and music equipment, in their woodworking class. If your kid builds his own storage he'll be more inclined to use it.**

strong statement

Teenage boys want to stamp their own personal style in their space just like girls. They too will respond best if you let them make their own choices. They typically enjoy anything with a rough, industrial edge, like chunky casters, ladders, or pulleys. They're also into gizmos and techno wizardry and will want to have the latest prize on display, so a prominent place for a music system or computer is essential. Teenage boys are renowned for being grungy and messy, but you can point them in the right direction with simple and in-their-face storage. Who knows, they might even start to use it.

ABOVE **Even if you're not short of garage space, don't stow it, show it. A bike can be stored overhead with a pulley system. It becomes a focal point and reinforces how different his taste is from yours.**

tip

A galvanized metal trash can with a large blackboard sign is more likely to succeed where a conventional laundry basket will definitely fail.

RIGHT **Use your space imaginatively and even a small room can become a teenager's haven. A raised sleeping platform is offbeat enough to appeal, and a desk and computer can tuck in below.**

BELOW **CDs can take over a music-crazy boy's room. Stack extra-large cardboard or plastic tubes, about one foot in length, in an alcove, one on top of the other, for this beehive storage. The CDs can then be sorted into bands or music styles in each nook.**

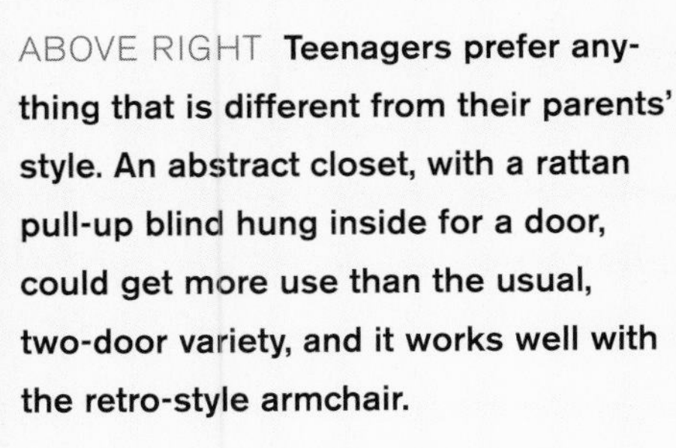

ABOVE RIGHT **Teenagers prefer anything that is different from their parents' style. An abstract closet, with a rattan pull-up blind hung inside for a door, could get more use than the usual, two-door variety, and it works well with the retro-style armchair.**

RIGHT **A coffee table just isn't on a teenage boy's wish list, but get him a durable one he can kick around, with chunky casters and a curvy shape, and he'll wonder how he managed before.**

events & gifts

tip

When planning your table, think about the style of dishware you have, and match it to the setting. A fine floral china dinner plate works best with crisp white linen or lace, while a rustic wooden platter will look wonderful against natural fabrics and hand-finished detail.

LEFT **A clear glass charger gives you an opportunity to adorn place settings individually. A scattering of two kinds of flower petals creates a delicate focus visible below each platter. The color of the tablecloth is key—the petals should stand out against the background.**

BELOW LEFT **There's no need to limit yourself to one place mat. Use layers to give each setting substance. Here, a green, braid-edged place mat is laid on top of a larger plain linen one, to which a border of tiny mirrors has been added. Smooth buttons sewn around the green mat create more texture and surface detail.**

extra touches

An important event demands a special tabletop, but with limited time for all the preparations, you'll want quick solutions that give the table instant impact. Your decorations can be a combination of reusable items like candles, vases, or place mats, with a one-time arrangement in the center tailored to the occasion. Include a few unexpected touches too—the element of surprise will add to the thrill. Whether it's a small dinner party or a larger gathering, one of the high points of a celebration is the first sight of the table decorated and laid with party fare. It takes only minimal preparation to make that a memorable moment.

BELOW **Crack open champagne and get the party going! Break away from a traditional chrome ice bucket and a stuffy atmosphere, using a capacious glass tank vase that puts the ice on show. Here, a denim table covering reflects the mix of clear and blue cubes for a young and exuberant flavor. Start making your colored ice a couple of days ahead of the event. Pour a solution of food coloring and water from a jug into ice trays and just pop them in the freezer.**

tip

Take great care that no colored ice falls on a carpet or upholstered furniture as it will stain. Serve colored ice at an event with a wooden or other hard, wipeable floor, or better still, save it for an outdoor event.

LEFT **Mini gift bags make an appealing change from the usual bread-basket or roll on a side plate, and can easily be reused. Buy a few in different patterns with colors that work as a group and with your table.**

RIGHT **Even ice cubes can become a way to add a novel element to your party. Fill a tray with water and float a single, washed mint leaf on each section. Gently push each one down so it is just under the water, but still flat and facing up. These are lovely added to refreshing summer drinks.**

hand-finished gifts

just for you

Handmade gifts really show people you've been thinking of them, but not everyone has the time to make a present from scratch. Add your own touches to personalize a store-bought item and you can still offer a gift that makes the recipient feel that little bit more special. Even the plainest inexpensive item can be transformed into a really thoughtful present with the right small embellishments. Don't worry that you're not the most talented artist—the simplest ideas are often highly effective. Using just basic art materials or inexpensive, everyday components you can give your item that extra lift that will set it apart from the crowd.

BELOW **Treasured family photos can get overhandled and damaged, so make a folding mini album for a relative. Scan or photocopy your pictures to preserve the originals, then, taking a strip of heavyweight paper, fold it accordian-style and weave a ribbon through a punched hole in the end panel. Use self-adhesive corner mounts to hold the photocopies in place. Tie the ribbon around the album to close it.**

ABOVE RIGHT **Make a luxurious present out of a modest perfume bottle using glass relief paint. This thick gold color comes in a tube with a fine nozzle for applying it. Practice first on scrap paper to feel how the paint flows. Choose a bottle with a clean shape and a simple design.**

BELOW RIGHT **Add a length of braid to a plain cushion and you've got an individual gift. A heart, held in place with a few stitches or a touch of fabric glue is an easy shape to make. Allow extra ribbon so some hangs loose at the crossover point. If you know the color scheme of the room in which your cushion will go, look for a cushion and trim that coordinate.**

BELOW You can easily improve on the plastic store packaging on a gift of bedding. Pull it off, and just pile up the folded bedding, tuck in your gift card, and tie it loosely in a stack, using liberal amounts of ribbon in two shades. Your present now has a sophistication and polish that a plastic bag could never give.

how to create an unusual plant display

Rather than wrapping a flowering plant in paper, present it ready for display in a glass fish-tank vase.

1. The stripes are created with orange lentils and green mung beans, whose tones complement the tangerine flower head and glossy dark green leaves of the plant. Take the plant out of its pot and put it in a small plastic bag. Pierce the bottom of the bag in several places to allow air to circulate around the roots.

2. Place the plant in a large glass tank. Use separate pitchers for the beans and lentils. Surround the plant with a deep layer of orange lentils, followed by a layer of mung beans. If the root-ball sits very close to the side of the vase, make a funnel from a sheet of paper to pour the beans right into the narrow gap. The layers need not be completely level—unevenness will make the stripes irregular and more visually interesting.

presents with presence

A gift basket is an entertaining way to customize a present. You'll have enormous fun handpicking the contents and tailoring them to the taste and interests of the recipient. Alternatively, a gift basket is a thoughtful way to offer items such as candles or soaps that are safe bets for someone whose tastes you don't know so well. The basket itself is key to the look of your gift—it might just be for presentation, holding perhaps cookies or preserves, or it could form part of the gift, like a pail filled with gardening goodies. Whatever you're packing it with, a shallow shape will show off the contents best. Complete the effect with an attractive filling material that relates to what's inside, like a pretty, scrunched-up fabric, wrapped candy, dried moss, or shredded colored tissue. Naturally a gift basket needs no wrapping, but do add a finishing touch, like a small bunch of lavender or some sprigs of rosemary, a beautiful bloom or a name tag that complements your gift in color or texture.

RIGHT **An avid gardener, or even an apartment-dweller with a window ledge, will enjoy an herb kit you've assembled yourself. A wide trug can hold several small terra-cotta pots, a mini watering can, and some seed packets. Perk up the pots by painting them different colors using masonry paints and nestle everything on a bed of dried moss.**

BELOW Luxury soaps are lovely to receive but can be exorbitantly expensive to give. Supermarket soaps, repackaged with a little imagination, will be equally appreciated. Take the soaps out of their existing packets and rewrap them neatly in an Asian newspaper. Tie each with a narrow scarlet ribbon. For a few dollars, buy a bamboo rice steamer and fill it with shredded black tissue for an original gift box inspired by the Far East.

LEFT Towels always make a welcome wedding or housewarming gift. Make yours stand out by displaying them in a basket instead of wrapping them up. Here towels in two shades of amethyst have been piled up and are held in place by a wide band of sapphire-blue satin ribbon, crowned with a single elegant lily flower. Remove the stamens of flowers to prevent pollen stains.

FAR LEFT Candles are part of so many people's evening routine, and in general a gift you can't go wrong with. Bundle each color together with a strip of gift wrap secured with a bow. Pick up a free wooden fruit crate at your local store, line it with velvet, dress the rough handles with a twist of ribbon, and pack the bundles in. The rough, functional look of the crate adds to its charm. Wrap a couple of matchboxes too, tucking a few spares into the ribbon, and fill in any gaps with single tea lights.

surprise trays

ABOVE **A desk tray complete with smart office accessories marks the first day in a new job or the start of college life. All the items are totally practical and are sure to be useful, but presented like this, they say so much more.**

ABOVE **Tea with scones and preserves is not an earth-shattering gift idea, but served up on a wicker tray lined in fresh-looking gingham they set the scene for an English summer tea party. Combine teapot and cups, scones, gingham-topped jars of preserves, and a small, simple vase of flowers.**

ABOVE **Soaps and toiletries are often well worth admiring, so welcome visitors with their own selection laid out on a tray in their room or the guest bathroom.**

serving it up

Put together a special tray to mark an occasion—it could be tea on Mother's Day, a birthday, or even a promotion at work. Whomever it's for will immediately feel loved and pampered. Even if the tray holds only an assortment of basic items like a cup of tea with homemade cookies or some new art materials for the start of the college semester, the thoughtful presentation will ensure a memorable moment. Pick your tray with care. It's the backdrop to the arrangement, setting the scene for making an insignificant event special. Depending on the occasion, you can line an existing tray with colored paper or patterned or textured fabric, or even scatter it with flower heads, confetti, or leaves.

BELOW **Served on a pretty tray, take-out Chinese food can be worth serving to company for a fun movie night. Line the tray with a folded sheet of Chinese newspaper, then rest the chopsticks on pristine bowls. Finish off with a lone, serene orchid blossom.**

FAR LEFT **An "emergency services" tray will cheer up anyone laid low with a cold. Use a bandage as a runner, wrap tissues in a red cross ribbon with a safety pin, and add a vitamin drink, a flower, and a shiny apple to keep the doctor away.**

LEFT **Raise the festivity level at any celebration with a cheerful tray. Serve drinks and snacks on a silver platter festooned with shiny streamers that invite guests to partake.**

gifted

The visual statement made by a wrapped present is an enormous part of the whole thrill of gift giving. An enticing parcel is a pleasure both to hand over and to open. The style of wrapping and the paper and trimmings you choose all say something about you but should also be appropriate to the person receiving the gift. The most effortless touches can make a present look incredibly irresistible, so take an extra few minutes to dress up the package. And think beyond traditional wrapping paper—alternatives like wallpaper, plain stationery paper, photocopies, and brown paper open up a whole range of possibilities.

ABOVE **A remnant of floral wallpaper and a sheet of plain white paper add up to fabulous packaging. Each one is trimmed with a ribbon, and fresh flowers tucked into the bows add that finishing touch.**

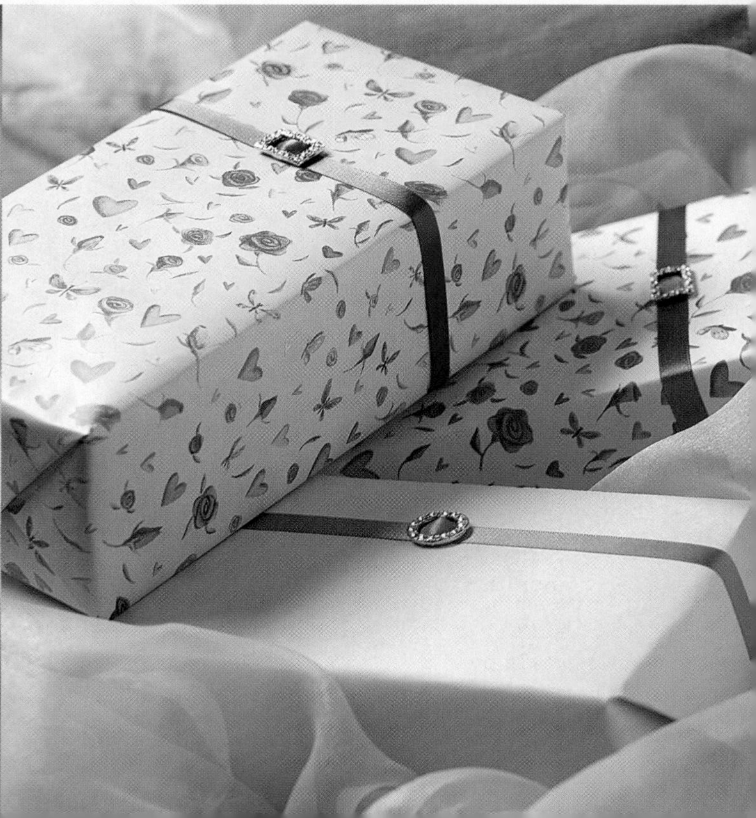

tip

Fresh flowers are only appropriate if you're able to give your gift within a couple of hours of wrapping, but sprigs of evergreen foliage or sturdy herbs such as rosemary will last longer. Make sure stems are thoroughly dry before they come into contact with the paper. Always secure your paper with double-sided adhesive tape tucked under the top layer—you'll achieve a smoother, more professional finish.

BELOW LEFT **A single, narrow band of contrasting satin, threaded with a tiny diamante buckle, has more style and sophistication than yards of multicolored ribbons, frills, and bows. Wound around the parcel and fixed underneath with double-sided tape, it's the perfect finishing touch.**

ABOVE RIGHT **Wrapping can frame a gift just as well as cover it. Fill a container with small clusters of flowers for guests to take away as they leave and let the bouquets speak for themselves. Surround each bunch in a sheet of greaseproof paper held in place with a chiffon bow and use informal little clips for name tags.**

RIGHT **Black and white is the ultimate in graphic chic, so for small parcels that are big on panache, try wrapping them with photocopies. Find an image you like, such as flowers or scenery, in a book or magazine, or make a montage of family pictures. If your package is larger than the size paper your photocopier can handle, you can attach two or more sheets together. Finish the present off with ribbons and bows, sticking with the monochromatic palette.**

invitations and tags

cordially invited

It's easy to buy preprinted invitations and gift tags for just about any occasion, but for really eye-catching cards that could only come from you, try making your own. You needn't spend hours on them—details like the color of your ink, the texture, and even the shape of the paper or card you choose will be enough to set yours apart from the rest. A beautiful or intriguing invitation is a special pleasure to receive—it gives a taste of what's to come and prompts your guests to look forward to the event as soon as they open it.

ABOVE **This feminine invitation would be well-suited to a bridal shower or wedding.**

how to make a buttoned invitation

A film of net fabric, held by a large fake mother-of-pearl button, enhances a paper invitation at minimal cost, adding glamour and texture.

1. **Handwrite your invitations or print them on a computer, using pearlescent paper. Leave the top third of the paper blank–this is where the button will go. Measure the paper, then mark out the shape on net fabric with a marker and a rigid ruler. Cut it out with sharp scissors.**
2. **Mark the center point of the top third of the paper with a tiny dot. Lay a piece of net exactly over the invitation. Thread a large needle with three strands of sparkly yarn, find the center mark, and push the needle from the front to the back of the paper leaving a couple of inches of yarn on the front, then through to the front again. Secure the button with a couple of stitches, then trim off either end of the yarn to end slightly longer than the width of the button, and remove the masking tape.**

ABOVE **With a little attention to detail, even packaged invitations can be distinguished and festive. Colored inks are so readily available, why stick with blue or black? Anything from red or purple to gold and silver can add to the look. Finish your envelopes with sealing wax—it lends a sense of importance to the contents and makes the whole experience of opening the invite so much more exciting.**

ABOVE **A bottle of wine is a common and much appreciated gift for the host, and adding a Christmas tree decoration to your wrapping paper at holiday time will set your bottle apart. Whatever the season or the occasion, a glittering ornamental tag will make more of your contribution and the event itself.**

RIGHT **Sheet-music scrolls, photocopied and singed at the edges, have all the party details printed inside, but even before they're unrolled you know the party theme. (See page 86 for the perfect place setting.)**

FAR RIGHT **Colored stationery is a great way to convey that a special event is on the horizon. Instead of everyday white, choose vivid scarlet envelopes, punched at one end and threaded with a tassel.**

christmas decorations

holiday cheer

Christmastime is a great opportunity to say no to run-of-the-mill, ready-made decorations and strike out on your own. You don't have to always start from scratch, though. Start with items like pre-sprayed twigs, then stir in your own sprinkling of personal creativity for a seasonal spectacular that no one else will have.

RIGHT **A garland of glossy pine fronds combined with inexpensive fruit and feathery painted twigs creates a natural and dramatic mantelpiece display. The white twigs seem to shoot out from the dark green, and the pears, painted with white latex paint, are a striking, organic touch. Choose the hardest unripened fruit you can find and it will last through the holiday.**

how to make a ribbon garland

This wicker wreath, dressed in frosty pastel chiffon ribbons, is a nice break from the traditional holiday colors and is incredibly easy to make.

1. Buy a wicker wreath from a florist, and chiffon ribbon in a variety of icy pinks, blues, lavenders, and greens.
2. Working around the circle, wrap and weave the ribbons one at a time. Tie the ends firmly onto the wreath at the back. As one color runs out, blend in the next and change the tones as you move around to achieve an iridescent effect. Choose a vibrant contrast color for the ribbon hanger.

LEFT Give a traditional tree a stress-free modern treatment and a subtle glow that reflects its surroundings. Arrange gold lights on the tree, then add in ready-sprayed gold twigs and willow-balls bought from a florist. Shorten the twigs nearer the top so they are graduated and seem almost like part of the tree. You may need to adjust the spread of lights once the twigs are inserted.

BELOW LEFT Advent envelopes will fast become a much-loved tradition and you can adapt the contents as the years go by. Fold in and pin the corners of precut felt squares to form envelopes. Thread a large needle with contrasting wool, secure the flaps with blanket stitch, and sew or paint on numbers from 1 to 24. Fill each one with a joke, a piece of candy, or trinket and place them among the fine twigs of a branch laid along a mantelpiece.

BELOW For an ornamental indoor wreath that won't eat too far into your budget, make your own. Buy a wire hoop from a florist, a length of silvery net fabric, and a selection of baubles in silver and turquoise. Wrap the fabric around the wire, then attach the decorations by threading a short strip of florist's wire through the top loop and fastening them to the wreath. This delicate contemporary version of a traditional Christmas decoration will bring a festive twinkle to your door year after year.

a warm glow

Candles are an integral part of Christmas. Nothing beats their gentle, flickering glow for setting the tone for both joyful celebrations and peaceful evenings. Before you start planning a candle display, decide where you want to position it. Beautiful though they are, naked flames can be devastatingly dangerous, so place them well away from children, pets, and any flammable materials like decorations, drapes, tablecloths or upholstery. A mantelpiece is an ideal spot, easy to see and enjoy, yet high enough to be out of reach. Put some sort of plate or tray underneath the candles to catch drips.

RIGHT AND FAR RIGHT **It couldn't be easier to give a bowl of floating candles an extra touch of glitter. Buy copper, silver, or gold leaf from a craft store, tear off tiny flakes and drop them on the water. Choose a wide container, allowing space for the leaf to float freely rather than crowding in too many candles. The copper finish of this dish increases the sense of glowing warmth.**

LEFT **Classic seasonal elements like candles and berries add up to a totally modern festive look. White cobbles interspersed with brilliant orange-red berries surround a row of five glass vases placed at regular intervals above this fireplace—simple to assemble but quite arresting. White sugar in the vases supports the candles.**

RIGHT **The natural sheen and intense redness of fresh cranberries make them a festive garnish. Unripe ones will last about three weeks. Using glass candleholders with a wider diameter than the candles, pour the berries into the base and around the top to create contrasting ruby bands.**

CENTER RIGHT **If you think wire pot-scrubbers are just for the kitchen sink, think again! These cleaning pads, usually composed of a knitted tube of fine gold or silver wire, cost very little, can be unraveled quite effortlessly, and have a crinkled surface that catches the light. Slip them over fat candles, encasing each in a shining mesh sleeve.**

BELOW RIGHT **Rout a circular section out of the top of beautiful logs for a pretty setting for tiny tea lights. Contain your display on a tray for safety, and add more tea lights, star-shaped thistle heads, and a stone bowl of wet moss. (Never use dried moss near flames.)**

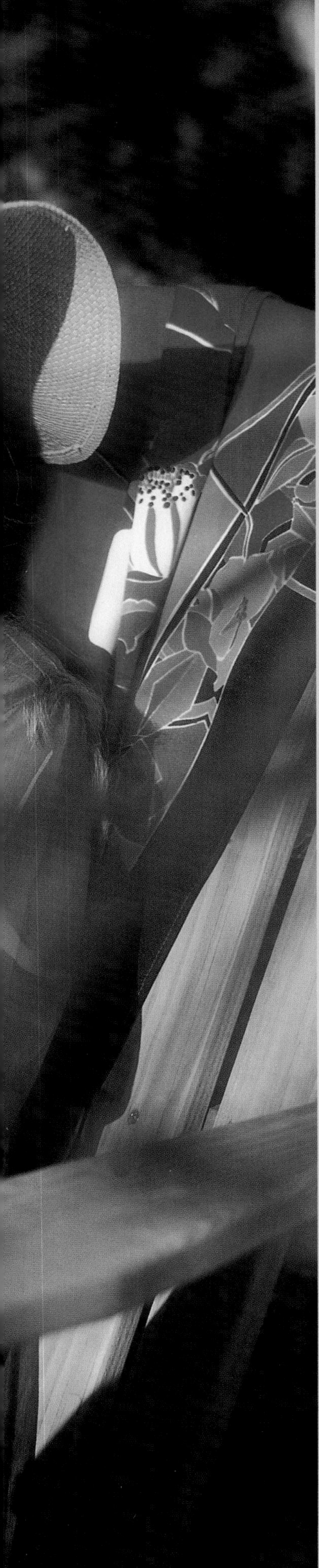

gardens

taking it easy

Relaxing outside in your garden should be as self-indulgent as you can make it, with furniture that feels as comfy as reclining in bed or as dreamy as snoozing on your sofa—your own perfect Eden. Whether you're dozing in the sun, reading in the shade, or entertaining friends for lunch, you need a selection of outdoor seating so you can enjoy your garden to the fullest. You might have a great vantage point for a simple bench overlooking a pond, the perfect big tree under which to hang a swing or lounger, and a selection of café-style chairs and a round table ideal for outdoor entertaining.

Tranquillity, comfort, and support are the priorities for seating. Think about making use of what's normally inside too: bring old or durable rugs outside, and cushions to ease a hard stone or wooden seat, so you can really enjoy the serenity. Your garden should be a peaceful sanctuary where you can take time out from the hustle and bustle of everyday life, but it'll only work if you have the right furniture.

ABOVE **Slung between handsome, shady trees in a peaceful part of the garden, a hammock is the ultimate in mellow living and a romantic accessory for the serious outdoor leisure-seeker.**

LEFT **Your garden needs plenty of sunlight, but you'll need some shade to be comfortable. Create some of your own with a simple, gauzy canopy over a cushion-strewn swinging bench or daybed.**

RIGHT **A contemporary, geometric glass table and stand, combined with natural slate seats, make a streamlined and chic statement in the garden. Clean shapes and hard materials suit a modern, minimalist look.**

BELOW Your garden doesn't close at dusk. Darkness will turn an outdoor sunken fireplace, surrounded by snug canvas chairs, into a hotspot for stargazing and chatting well into the night.

BOTTOM For a complete outdoor switch-off from the daily grind, you need good ergonomics—comfort, bolstering, and somewhere to set an iced drink or a novel. Traditional wooden Adirondack chairs are made for the job.

ABOVE Have you noticed how much better food seems to taste outside? Café-style, contemporary metal furniture sets the tone for an al fresco breakfast or refreshing mid-afternoon drink. It's ideal for a terrace if space is tight.

ABOVE RIGHT Use painted wooden seating to add year-round cheer. The natural world is bursting with a cocktail of hues, so why not go for colors really evocative of summer on a traditional wood and wrought-iron bench?

pots and baskets

spruced up

You really don't need to splurge on expensive, exotic, or unusual plants to create an outstanding display in your garden. In the right setting, the commonest grasses, bulbs, herbs, or flowering annuals will translate into an exciting exhibit. Spend a bit of time experimenting with containers as combinations of height, shape, color, and texture all affect the look. It's not just the containers themselves but also where you place them that's important. By grouping a collection of pots together you can go for high impact with the most humble containers. Give some thought to top dressing, too. Earth is okay, but a surprising contrast will create far more excitement. Containers are much more than just accessories to plants, and as any well-dressed person will tell you, accessories are what usually turn a simple outfit into something stunning.

TOP **Recycled old car tires, primed and painted with outdoor-quality paints, are superb for growing strawberries or herbs. They're unbreakable and the kids will love them!**

ABOVE **A series of streamlined pots and a handful of spartan white gravel can make the simplest of variegated grasses look architectural.**

tip

No more dreary baskets! Add some chandelier crystal drops that sway in the breeze, gleam in the sunlight, and transform a routine hanging basket into a special feature with personality.

LEFT Containers can become part of your garden display, spicing up what's happening on the ground. Color, shape, and structure are what you notice here, while the plants themselves are merely a finishing touch.

ABOVE LEFT The right containers can make or break a strong visual statement. Set against an eye-popping orange wall and planted with trend-setting black-stemmed bamboos, carefully chosen, large galvanized metal containers reinforce a very modern look.

ABOVE RIGHT Even a plain terra-cotta pot has no excuse for looking uninteresting. Seek out pleasing shapes and add your own special personal touch, like an intricate painted detail.

how to paint a pot

Paint is the quickest and most reliable way of introducing color—both indoors and out. Create as many different designs as you like, using masonry paints on terra-cotta pots, but keep to a palette of three or four accent shades to give your grouping some structure.

1. Thoroughly clean and dry the terra-cotta pot. Paint the pot using a suitable masonry paint. Allow it to dry.
2. Mask off the desired shapes using masking tape. Paint the masked-off area. Remove masking tape while the paint is still a little tacky. Allow to dry.

ground cover

style underfoot

The biggest single area in your garden is the ground, and it's crying out for design. Whether you want a natural wilderness or a Spanish-style courtyard, what's underfoot really sets the scene. Cobbles, gravel, paving, and wood can dress the ground in patterns and textures, while guiding your eye to the best features. To get the most from the garden all year around look at everything from tiles to outdoor paints. Think practicalities, too. Who's using the garden? Kids and pets just won't appreciate hard, unforgiving surfaces or fragile plants. How much work are you really prepared to do? Grass is great, but too much may not be the best option if you're hoping for a high-relaxation, low-maintenance garden. Whatever budget or time restrictions you might have, there's a profusion of choices to explore, and ground cover merits great care and attention. So get right down to ground level and don't be left standing with (or on) humdrum choices.

ABOVE **Simple touches are often the most successful. The plainest blond wood decking, dressed up with inserted parallel galvanized metal bands, has modest presence and impact.**

how to paint concrete paving slabs

Concrete paving slabs are fairly elementary, but outdoor floor paints in glorious colors will work wonders. Two striking shades and a delicate dragonfly stencil take concrete into a gracious new realm.

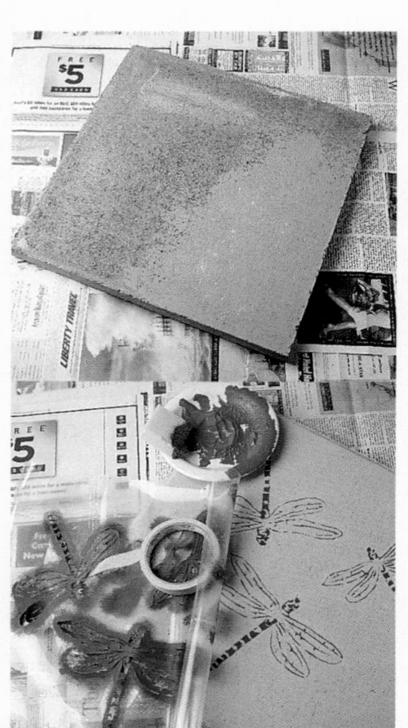

1. **Paint the paving slabs using an exterior flooring paint suitable for concrete. Allow them to dry.**
2. **Secure the stencil in place using masking tape. Pour some paint into a small dish. Dip a small sponge into the paint and remove the excess by rubbing the sponge on scrap newspaper to make sure it's not loaded too heavily with paint. Gently dab the sponge on the stencil until the required depth of color is achieved. Remove stencil. Allow to dry.**

ABOVE **The lizard mosaic heralds entry to the Spanish-inspired garden.**

BELOW **Offset an intricate mosaic tile panel with budget-priced, tactile wooden blocks cut from fencing posts and treated with preservative and a distinctive pale gravel in a geometric layout.**

ABOVE **Hard materials like cobblestones and recycled glass gravel work best interspersed with minimalist planting. Low-growing feathery grasses or velvety silver foliage seem sculptural set against an unusual ground cover.**

ABOVE **With flame-colored flowers, forget an earth or gravel mulch and use a remarkable backdrop of sheeny, black barbecue coals.**

BELOW LEFT AND BELOW **A mix of materials turns a sad patch into a stylish path. Wooden decking squares combined with cobbles create a maintenance-free zone.**

tip

Rework a classic material. Fenceposts sliced and treated with preservative deliver rustic ground cover with a difference. Keep the area weed-free by filling the gaps with gravel in a contrasting tone.

points of interest

It's not just plants that can energize your garden and give it real charisma. Special features are the secret to making sure that whether you are meandering along a path, lounging in a deck chair, or eating lunch with the family, there's always something exciting to feast your eyes on. Garden features can be anywhere—down on the ground, at eye level, or above your head. You might choose something substantial and practical, like a small, pretty summerhouse or an unusual bridge over a stream. Alternatively, you could shine the spotlight on a beautiful mosaic pot, a delightful little object. For height and shape, and if you can wait for them to grow, flowering climbers like honeysuckle or clematis seem jewel-like trained over an arch or pergola, though their beauty is seasonal. If you want year-round interest, go for more permanent solutions. Stone, pots, and wood, plus a little wit and childish imagination, are excellent vehicles for unusual additions to your outdoor space. With some thought and creativity, a winter garden can have color and a newly planted plot instant shape and variety of height.

ABOVE LEFT AND CENTER LEFT **A summerhouse can provide theater, comfort, and a bold splash of color. A subdued blue combined with an oxidized roof allows the structure at the top to blend in with its surroundings, while in the center the dramatic muslin drapes demand attention, providing a perfect vehicle for lively al fresco entertaining.**

LEFT AND RIGHT **Structural forms give weight and structure to a garden design. Items such as willow obelisks, stacked naturally shapped stones, and ceramic spheres in cobalt and blue give any lackluster garden bed an instant touch of the extraordinary.**

ABOVE LEFT **Why just go for a straightforward plank of wood? A bridge that curves and delights with a three-way split transforms the established link needed from one part of the garden to another.**

LEFT **Make a break in a mammoth expanse of paving—throw in an ambitious, detailed inset compass design that accentuates the location.**

ABOVE CENTER **A weathered, old upturned wooden boat that looks as though it just floated in on the tide can be metamorphosed into an idyllic setting for a flower-child flower pot arrangement.**

ABOVE **A bridge doesn't have to go over water. It could simply be introduced as an artistic vehicle that leads from one place to another, breaking the monotony of a flat garden layout, with a place to pause for thought.**

tip

A single arch planted with climbers will excite you only so far, so position and plant enough to create a luscious leafy tunnel and a truly green garden experience.

final flourishes

Details are the lipstick and mascara, the tie and cufflinks, that complete your garden, adding that extra layer of style and polish. Details won't stop you in your tracks; they are the small surprises and unexpected touches you'll stumble on almost by chance. Your garden could easily be a bigger space than any room inside your home, and the selection of looks to choose from is endless, but don't let that intimidate you. Check your self-doubt at the door, and have some fun thinking about the small details alongside the larger, focal structures. You'll soon start to see the overall picture taking shape. Keep details simple—they'll have more impact. Masses of fussy pieces or too much variety just spell confusion, so stick to key materials that work with everything else in the space. Remember, getting the details right will enhance the whole experience.

ABOVE **A natural rope stepping-stone, coiled and laid over rough cobbles, instantly gives you the flavor of the beach and leaves familiar concrete slabs in the dust. The rope has been coiled onto a disk of marine ply and tacked into place with hidden nails.**

RIGHT **Even if the spotlight falls squarely on the plants, make sure the rest of the bed is up to standard. Look out for inexpensive, unusual edging like recycled, ribbed terra-cotta drainpipes to finish the picture perfectly.**

tip

Words will definitely give your herb pots extra panache. Use masonry paints and stencils to achieve this with ease.

ABOVE LEFT **A richly colored Japanese maple tree, bedded in a glazed ceramic pot with a top layer of cobalt-blue glass gravel, becomes a complete color statement with more zing than plain, brown earth would give you.**

ABOVE **Wind chimes hung from a tree gleam in the sunlight and make subtle background tones that will soothe and relax you as they sway in the breeze.**

CENTER LEFT **The risers of your steps don't get walked on, but since they are the most prominent part why not decorate them with Spanish-inspired glazed, patterned tiles? Use resilient terra-cotta tiles on the treads to withstand foot traffic.**

LEFT **A striking sculpture can be even more special when it's not placed center stage. Surprise explorers by hiding it in a flower bed to add an extra dimension just off the main drag.**

go with the flow

The presence of water in a garden is extraordinary. It makes a breathtaking living element that you can't beat for beauty, whether sparkling in a falling stream or as a still, reflective pool. Who can resist holding their hand under a cool fountain on a sweltering day? Water can create the most soothing sounds in the world, though it pays to get the noise level and tone just right. Water is great fun, too. Kids adore messing around with pools and waterfalls (although you must be aware of the dangers of water for youngsters). A garden pond or even a birdbath will attract all kinds of wild visitors like frogs, insects, butterflies, and birds. No matter how small or awkward your space, water will really make your garden flow and come to life.

ABOVE **Water can become part of a larger garden feature as its natural flow, cascading from one level to another, adds a feeling of movement. Throw in handfuls of blue glass and aluminum gravel for extra highlights.**

ABOVE **With a simple pump mechanism, your water feature can be mobile. Here, water flows around a potted plant within the larger, ribbed terra-cotta pot.**

BELOW LEFT **The simplest fountain spout, made from copper piping and set in a formal, tiled pool, can become the star attraction of a large, paved terrace.**

ABOVE CENTER **Look for water accessories with interesting sculptural shapes that make them beautiful objects in their own right. A series of attractive copper cups catch the water and overflow to the next level.**

ABOVE **Water never fails to fascinate. A cast terra-cotta face is completely hidden from the front by a wide cascade. From the side it's clearly seen beneath a wafer-thin sheet of water.**

LEFT **The smallest space can still be host to a stunning water feature. This low-level Japanese-inspired pool, studded with pebbles and encased in shards of natural riven slate, is softened at the edges with delicate ferns.**

al fresco

Eating in the garden is a joy. Fresh air and green surroundings do such wonders for the smell, taste, and total pleasure of food that there's no need to try too hard with the table. Don't wear yourself out attempting to re-create a formal dining room in your garden. Space will be limited, cloths and napkins will blow around, insects will hover, and instead of relaxing you'll be rushing indoors for missing items that no one really needs. Stay cool and serene by keeping decorative touches natural and uncomplicated. Picnic plates and thermoses are portable, practical, and add to the ease and special atmosphere of outdoor meals. Reduce mess and cleanup with disposable alternatives such as paper or nontoxic leaves for serving all sorts of snacks and finger foods. Decorate napkins or plates with minimal effort. Just use a single flower or sprig of greenery for a gorgeous natural touch that only lasts the day.

TOP RIGHT **The simplest, most effortless decorative touches work best outside. It takes no time to tie a flower onto a napkin or around the rim of a glass. Leftover bottles of different sizes and shades make handy groups of vases for single stems.**

CENTER RIGHT **A mat of white coiled rope may not be appropriate indoors but is perfect for a casual drink in the garden. Avoid return trips indoors for more coffee or iced drinks by bringing a cooler or thermoses out.**

RIGHT **Jam jars with mirrored sequins and ribbon glue-gunned in place make instant candleholders that can be changed seasonally or given a theme for a party or event.**

RIGHT **Roll colored writing paper, lined with a sheet of wax paper, into a cone—the perfect outdoor, no-wash plate for hot, salty popcorn, barbecued vegetables, or baked rosemary potatoes.**

ABOVE **Make fun, throwaway place mats out of cardboard. Here, a naïve plate and cutlery have been painted for a whimsical dining setting. Why not get the kids to give it a try? Make sure to use paints that are safe to eat off of.**

tip

Insects can ruin a peaceful snack on a hot day. A small handkerchief, edged with beading that gives the weight needed to keep it in place, will stop the bees dipping into your jam, lemonade, or fruit.

how to paint a room

Preparation is the key to any good painting job. I recommend that you use acrylic or water-based paints. Not only do they dry quickly, but they are kinder to the environment.

1. **Clothing.** Wear cotton clothes that you don't mind getting paint on. Don't wear wool, because lint will stick to the paint. If you've got long hair, wear a cap or tie it up. Wear loose-fitting rubber gloves to protect your hands and nails.

2. Empty the room of all accessories: books, CDs, television set, VCR, pictures, curtains, blinds, ornaments, rugs, and the like. Move all of the remaining furniture into the center of the room. Cover the furniture with protective plastic sheets and tape them down to the floor. Run a strip of masking tape all around the edge of the room at the bottom of the baseboards to protect the floor. Cover the remaining exposed floor space with plastic sheets, tape them down, and then lay cotton drop cloths on top. Don't leave anything uncovered—you'll regret it later!

3. Slightly loosen all electric switch plates so there is a small gap between them and the wall surface. Cover the entire switch plate with masking tape.

4. Remove flaking paint, loose plaster, or wallpaper. Remove flaking paint with a scraper, then lightly sand the area to smooth the surface. The most effective way of removing wallpaper is to rent a wallpaper stripper from your local home improvement store. They are easy to use and come with full instructions.

5. Fill any holes, cracks, or nicks. Somewhat enlarge the holes or cracks to remove any loose plaster. Use spackle to fill in small cracks and nicks. Use plaster for larger areas. Large areas or new walls of fresh plaster will need to be primed.

6. Sand any newly filled areas to a smooth finish. Sand down all woodwork. Also sand down surfaces that do not have an existing painted surface, such as kitchen cabinet doors or surfaces with a synthetic finish. (By sanding the area, you create a surface that the paint will adhere to.) If you are going to paint a wooden floor, sand it using a floor sander, which can be rented from a home improvement or hardware store.

7. Vacuum up all the dust. Wipe all surfaces clean with damp, lint-free cloths to ensure that you've removed all dust before painting.

8. Set out the paint cans on a piece of flattened cardboard on top of your drop cloths, for extra protection against spills. Use matte latex paint on the ceiling and walls and acrylic eggshell on the window frames, doors, and baseboards. Keep all rollers, brushes, and tools in another cardboard box so you can locate everything easily.

9. Always stir the paint thoroughly for about two minutes before using it straight from the can or pouring it into a paint tray.

10. Dip the paintbrush into the paint until the paint is halfway up the bristles. Never get paint on the metal band of the brush. Dab the brush against the inside of the container to ensure that the bristles are completely soaked in paint. Remove excess paint by dragging the bristles across the inside lip of the container.

11. **Ceiling.** Start with the ceiling. Use a brush to paint a strip around the edges of the ceiling where it meets the wall. Next, paint around any light fittings that are on the ceiling. This is called *cutting in.*

12. Pour paint into the deep end of the paint tray to within a half inch of the flat edge, which should be left free of paint. Dip the roller into the paint and rotate it by pushing it against the edge of the flat surface so that it gets fully loaded with paint. Next, move the roller back and forth across the flat surface of the paint tray to remove any excess paint. You're ready when the roller is full of paint but doesn't drip when you lift it up. You'll need to use an extension pole attachment or a ladder to reach the ceiling.

13. Start in a corner, carefully rolling along a small section of the line that you've cut in. Roll a V shape and paint up and down and back and forth until the area is evenly covered in paint. Remember, if the roller gets too dry you'll end up pulling the wet paint off the ceiling. Work from one end of the room to the other.

14. **Walls.** Once the ceiling is dry, cut in around the edges of the walls, ceiling, baseboards, doors, windows, switch plates, and joins where walls meet—anywhere that might be awkward for a roller to reach.

15. Roller the walls in the same way as you did the ceiling, starting at the top of the wall and working your way down. Never take a break when you're halfway through painting a wall. Finish the whole wall; otherwise, when the paint is dry, you'll see a faint line where you stopped.

16. **Windows.** Prime the original woodwork with acrylic primer to act as an undercoat for the acrylic eggshell top coat. Start by cutting in around the edge of the glass and working your way outward. Don't load your brush with too much paint. Brush out well. During painting, move any movable sections to ensure that they don't jam or end up being sealed shut. Use a blade to clean any paint off the glass.

17. **Doors.** Follow the instructions for windows.

18. **Floors.** When all the paint is dry, remove all furniture and drop cloths from the room and thoroughly vacuum the floor. Complete cover floor paint can be applied directly onto wood or concrete floors. Cork, vinyl, and linoleum will need to be primed first using acrylic primer. Test a small area first to ensure that the flooring will take the primer, since some types of cork, vinyl, and linoleum can't be painted. Acrylic floor wood glaze can be applied directly onto a sanded wooden floor. Apply at least three coats and leave overnight to dry before heavy use.

19. **Baseboards.** Wipe down the baseboards before you paint them—they'll have gathered dust and particles while the ceiling, walls, windows, and doors were being painted. Use masking tape to protect the bottom of the wall where it meets the baseboard. You should have already masked off the flooring along the edge of the baseboards before you put the drop cloths down.

20. Clean hands and tools with warm, soapy water. Always keep samples of the paint for touch-up jobs. Write on the container lid with a felt-tip pen what the paint was used for. Don't place anything on windowsills or shelves for a month after painting, until the paint has "cured." Walls can be wiped clean after a month using a nonabrasive detergent diluted in water.

hand care

10 Tips for Fabulous Hands

Your hands say so much about you, yet when it comes to looking after them while doing home renovation, we often forget to give them the basic care required to keep them looking good. Here are my tips to maintaining great hands and nails while still doing everything else around the house.

1. Never, ever use your nails as tools! Even the healthiest and strongest nails shouldn't be levering or scraping things. Instead find the right tool for the job.

2. Always wear larger than necessary rubber gloves when doing any decorating. This will allow your hands to breathe more easily and make it easier to slip the gloves on and off when they're covered in paint. Don't forget to wear gloves for preparation, too, such as stripping, sanding, and filling. If moisture builds up inside the gloves, then wear a pair of thin cotton ones underneath. Gardening gloves are a must when working outside, so don't be tempted to pull them off.

3. Ensure that you use only acetone-free nail polish remover. Acetone leaves the nails very dry and more susceptible to breakage.

4. After washing your hands, rinse them well and dry them carefully, so no dampness is left that can lead to chapping or rough skin.

5. Use a good-quality hand cream, which needs to be rubbed into the skin and nails as often as you can, at least three times a day.

6. Every few days treat your nails to an oil bath. Soak them in a small bowl of mineral or vegetable oil for ten minutes, then wipe the oil away with cotton balls.

7. Once a week lavishly apply an intensive hand cream, pull on cotton gloves, and relax for thirty minutes while watching your favorite TV show.

8. Use good-quality emery boards, not metal files. Use a medium grade to shorten and a fine grade to smooth edges or remove any snags.

9. Nails filed in a squarer shape have stronger edges than oval tapered shapes.

10. Polish helps protect nails from wear and tear. Use a base coat polish before applying a top coat in the color of your choice. Finish off with a clear top coat. Be sure to let each coat dry properly.

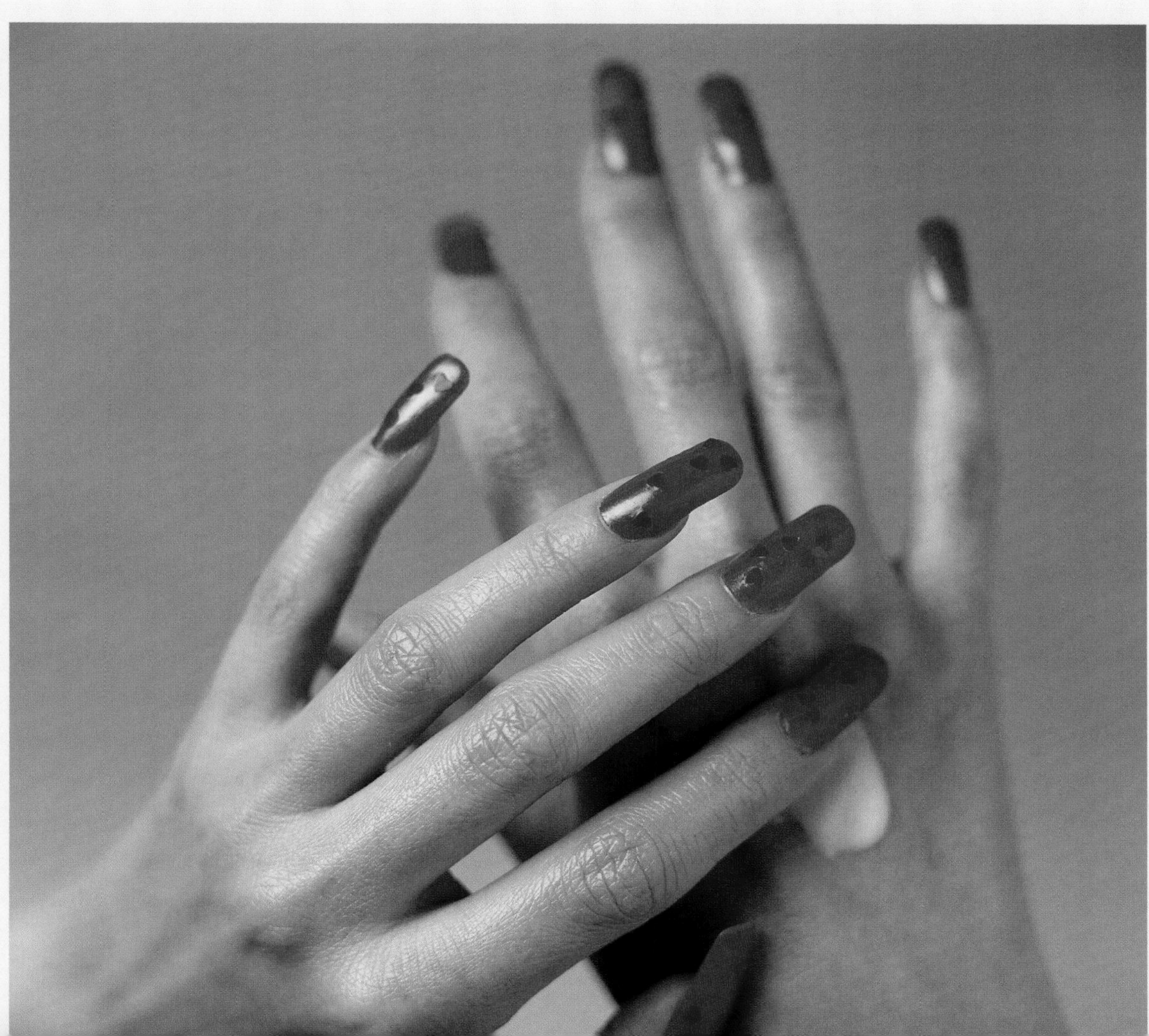

credits

Photography © 1996, 1997, 1998, 1999 by Anne McKevitt and © 2000, 2001, 2002 by Anne McKevitt Ideas.

All photographs herein depict the interior design work of Anne McKevitt unless otherwise stated.

All photography by Colin Poole except:

Photography by Anne McKevitt, pages 17 (top right and center right), 113 (top right), 155 (bottom right), 159 (bottom left and top center), 160 (top left and center left), 161 (bottom left and top right), 163 (bottom left and top right), 164 (bottom left), 165 (top left, top center, and bottom).

Thanks to Anne McKevitt Ideas paint PR for pages 1, 18 (top left), and 126 (bottom center). Photographs by Nick Pope.

Thanks to Chris Wood for page 110 (top left).

Thanks to Wickes and Michael Kamlish at Direct Communications for page 110 (bottom left).

Page 165 (bottom) designed by Fumiyaki Takano and photographed at Chaumont-sur-Loire, France.

A special thank you to the Royal Horticultural Society for giving Anne permission to photograph at various Hampton Court and Chelsea flower shows in London and to the following designers whose stunning work Anne has photographed:

Shani Lawrence and Katie Waller, pages 154 (left) and 160 (bottom left).

Mark Davis, pages 154 (top) and 161 (top left and top right).

Patrick Clarke and Patrick Wynniatt-Hussey, pages 155 (bottom left) and 157 (top center).

Guy Farthing, page 155 (center right).

Susanna Brown, pages 155 (top left) and 156 (center right).

James Basson, pages 156 (top right), 161 (top center), and 163 (center left).

David Burm, pages 157 (top right), 159 (top left), 163 (center right), and 164 (bottom right).

Jeremy Salt and Roger Bullock, pages 159 (top right) and 165 (top right).

A.B. Landscapes, page 159 (bottom left).

Karen Maskell, page 159 (center left).

Christopher Costin, pages 160 (top left) and 165 (top center).

Jane Rendell and Sarah Tavender, page 160 (center left).

Alan Gardner, page 161 (center left).

Land Art, page 161 (bottom right).

Cherry Burton, page 163 (bottom).

Thanks to the following companies for supplying products featured in the Gardens chapter:

Adirondack
garden chairs
tel: 44-1932-352-038

Dandf Design
decking
tel: 44-1977-704-796

Garden Pride
wicker obelisks
tel: 44-1273-440-552

Nonington Pottery
water cascade
tel: 44-1304-840-174

Specialist Aggregates
glass gravel
tel: 44-1785-665-554

Stewart Lotus
ribbed terra-cotta water feature
tel: 44-20-8686-2231

Windmill Aggregate
glass gravel
tel: 44-1785-661-018

index

that's
all for
now...